Anne Cawood

toddlers need
BOUNDARIES

Effective discipline without punishment

Anne Cawood

toddlers need BOUNDARIES

Effective discipline without punishment

METZ PRESS ▇

DEDICATION

This book is dedicated to my mother, Elizabeth Swift, who had to adjust to the challenges of parenting at such a young age – and did it so well.

Published by Metz Press
1 Cameronians Avenue, Welgemoed, 7530 South Africa

First published in 2009
Reprinted in 2012, 2013

Publisher	Wilsia Metz
Copy editing	Christopher & Deborah Morbin
Proofreader	Lesley Howard
Design & layout	Liezl Maree, Blue Berry Advertising
Illustrations	Lance Khoury
Cover photographs	Ivan Naudé

Printed and bound Mega Digital, Parow Industria
ISBN 978-1-920268-21-3

Acknowledgements

Once again, an enormous vote of thanks to my husband, Mike, for his patient interpretation of my illegible handwriting and the many hours spent converting my hand-written notes into a manuscript. Also for remaining so enthusiastic and interested in yet another book on the topic of children and boundaries – without you it would have been a very lonely and difficult task. It has been such fun doing these books together!

I would never have been empowered to give advice to other parents on the daunting issues of parenting toddlers had I not had four children (and then four grandchildren!) on whom to practise. I am therefore indebted to my now grown-up children, Catherine Shaw, Samantha-Jane Gale, Carolyn and Gregory Cawood, as well as grandchildren, Megan and Bronwen Shaw and Emily and Oliver Gale. An extra special thank you to those of you who were typical, challenging and determined toddlers (you know who you are!) and to all of you for surviving my attempts at effective parenting and for not giving up on me. Each one of you has contributed to my knowledge and understanding of this very challenging life-stage and for this, I am sincerely grateful.

A very special vote of thanks must go to my former colleagues at The Parent Centre in Cape Town, who offered so much support, guidance and friendship during those early days of our Mother and Toddler Workshops and coffee mornings. A special mention must be made of my friends and colleagues, Jenny Mackay and Lilian Giddey. We learnt so much during our days of developing and running groups and workshops for parents of babies and toddlers.

Of course, nothing would have been possible without all those babies, toddlers and their parents who helped us to hone our skills and fully understand the complex challenges for parents and toddlers during the stage of toddlerhood. Since going into private practice, I have been given the opportunity to remain in touch with the challenges of toddlerhood by the many parents who have turned to me for advice and support. Thank you for your trust in my input and opinions.

Finally, my thanks go to my aunt, Paddy Harrison, for the wonderful venue at her St James seaside home (so conducive to putting experience and opinion into writing) and for her ongoing support of my literary endeavours. And, as always, to my publisher, Wilsia Metz and the incredible team connected with Metz Press, including Monean Winterbach: it is a pleasure working with all of you.

Contents

Introduction

When I wrote my first book, *Children Need Boundaries*, it aimed to cover the very vital issue of the differences between effective discipline and the out-dated tendency to equate discipline with punishment. The book was broad in scope and covered all the developmental stages from birth to adolescence. I was gratified at the enthusiasm with which the book was received, but it almost immediately opened up doors for more in-depth discussion of the various stages. Adolescence definitely needed more attention than the rather cursory overview given in the first book. As a result, this led to my second book, *Teenagers Need Boundaries*. Simultaneously though, more and more of the questions asked at talks, workshops, in individual counselling and on the Media 24 Parenting web-page, indicated the need to pay more detailed attention to the very vital baby and toddler stages.

Two of my fellow Metz Press authors, Megan Faure and Ann Richardson, have written the best-selling books, *Baby Sense* and *Toddler Sense*, which make vital reading for parents of young children. Yet another Metz Press publication, *Positive Parenting*, by Margaret Fourie also offers excellent insight into the challenges of parenting children of all ages. So why then the need for this, a third book, in the 'Boundaries' series? Mainly because as a social worker, school counsellor, parenting counsellor and educator, mother and grandmother, I have personally experienced the struggle parents have in their attempts to translate theory into practice. Most parents today sincerely wish to move away from the autocratic, harsh and punitive parenting methods of yesteryear, yet find it difficult to put their theories into practice when confronted with real-life, acting-out children. It has also become more and more obvious to me that the early childhood stages really *do* set the scene for all the later stages. So many problems could be avoided or, at least, minimized if only parents could develop a more positive understanding of how to effectively parent, and therefore also to discipline, their toddlers.

I am confronted daily by parents, grandparents, teachers and carers who ask questions like: "I manage to stay calm and consistent when I've had a good day, but what can I do when I'm stressed and the kids are tired and demanding? Then it all goes out of the window." Or, "I'm really battling. I don't want to smack, but I ask calmly several times, count to five, try to reason with this impossible child and then finally resort to a smack. Is this really so bad? At least the child then listens!" Often I hear, "Please help me, I can never think of a reasonable consequence for an out-of-control three-year-old?" Then there was, "Surely a smack on the bottom (over the nappy) can do no harm at this stage?"

All these – and many, many more similar questions and concerns – nudged me towards the realisation that my Parenting Boundaries Series **had** to include a thorough and very practical 'tool kit' for the parents of younger children. As was the case with the teens book, there is clearly a need for one on toddlers.

This book does not replace *Children Need Boundaries*, which is a necessary precursor to a more 'specialist' book. The first one deals with the mindset changes needed in order to move from entrenched views and myths around the whole question of discipline, which will not be covered in as much detail in this book. Therefore, *Toddlers Need Boundaries* builds on the firm foundations established in that first one.

Although it is specifically aimed at the toddler stage, the first two chapters will deal with the adjustment to parenthood and the beginnings of discipline during the baby stage. In Chapter 3, I will handle the transition from babyhood to toddlerhood. I have included an overview of the baby stage because so much of how the baby emerges from this stage into toddlerhood depends upon how parents have handled the adjustment process.

After looking at the emergence into the toddler stage, I take a 'breather' in Chapter 4 to remind the parents of toddlers that they too need to re-establish their own individual and relationship boundaries. This is crucial to their handling of the challenges awaiting them when their toddlers begin asserting themselves.

As I begin this third book, I am excited at the prospect of the challenges that lie ahead, as I truly believe that the toddler stage is the most crucial for the establishment of future, positive, parent-child communication and long-term emotionally healthy relationships.

Let's begin at the beginning …

1

The adjustment to parenting

AND BABY MAKES 3 (OR 4 OR 5!)

That moment when you finally hold your brand new baby in your arms, when you finally gaze at this miracle, which is a wonderful and unique extension of each of you, something incredible takes place and you are overcome with the enormity of the moment. It is no longer just the two of you: from now on this little bundle of needs and demands is an integral part of your lives, which have changed completely. As with any momentous event, there is so much that is positive, exciting and challenging. At the same time though, you cannot have a positive without at least some kind of inevitable negative. This is the major problem for so many parents: the positives are stressed (as they should be) and everyone is thrilled and delighted. The flowers, presents and cards are exciting, grandparents are over the moon and, at last, the nursery has a baby to complete it. And then the inevitable happens – no one mentioned anything about the fact that after the euphoria and excitement, there has to be a downside. You realize that you may have 'gained' a beautiful baby but this is accompanied by a certain amount of losses too: sleep, 'me' and 'us' time, and income, to name but a few. It can arrive like a bolt out of the blue and, unless effectively dealt with, can lead to ongoing communication problems. Hence the need to spend some time reviewing this before tackling the actual toddler issues. After all, if the adjustment process has been flawed, the 'baggage' of the unresolved issues will contaminate the effectiveness of parenting your toddler positively.

> *"Every set of parents, I believe, goes through a crisis. Birth is a crisis, and a lot of them don't deal very well with that crisis; they don't even realize it is a crisis."*
> Alison Osborne: *The Post-baby Conversation: What new parents need to say to each other*

For this reason, it is vital to spend some time reviewing the transition from childless couple to a couple with a child. This is most definitely a life-changing event and, like any traumatic life experience, needs a very skilled adjustment process. The fact is, however, that for two of the most demanding and far-reaching roles of our lives, we have absolutely no formal training: being an adult, intimate relationships and becoming parents. When we are physically ill, we go to the relevant doctor but how many of us turn to the relevant 'doctor' when we encounter emotional or relationship problems? The truth is that many adults view these as weaknesses. I am asked, "But why should I discuss my personal issues with a stranger?" Or, "My parents managed fine without courses, workshops, counselling and books on how to relate to partners and children, so why should we need these in order to cope?"

The answers are simple:

- They did not cope all *that* well. Witness the problems we see today, such as high divorce rates etc.
- Society has changed: children know their rights and are, thankfully, more assertive.
- We do not instinctively know how to communicate, especially when life throws curved balls at us.

Were you really prepared for it?

No matter how 'longed-for' that first baby is, how many of you were truly prepared for the enormity of becoming parents for the first time? By the same token, how many of you would have believed how life changing it would prove to be?

I have often asked audiences, groups and individuals if they could ever have been adequately prepared for the physical, social and emotional changes that one tiny bundle of needs and demands would evoke in their lives. The consensus of opinion has always been that not even a degree in parenting would be sufficient preparation and most of us have absolutely no training!

Psychologists who have made a study of stressful life-events equate the birth of a baby (especially the first) to negative events such as divorce and death. Parents are horrified when confronted with this fact but, upon reflection, concur that it is indeed a traumatic and life-changing event.

BUT LET'S GO BACK TO THE *VERY* BEGINNING

As young adults, we fall in love and commit to long-term relationships. During those early days of magnetic attraction, spontaneous fun, spur-of-the-moment decisions and interpersonal bonding, how many couples sit down and discuss their views on parenting roles, discipline methods and expectations of each other in the future?

Usually, the only parenting 'skills' we bring to the relationship are the ones our parents used on us and, no matter how idyllic our childhood may have been, the methods used 25 years ago will, in all likelihood, not be entirely applicable in raising children in the 21st century.

Couples commit to each other and those early, relaxed, one-on-one days unfold: lovely, lazy Sunday mornings in bed with coffee, croissants and the newspapers. There are the romantic, candlelit suppers with red wine and uninterrupted conversations, or long, leisurely walks with nothing to worry about apart from perhaps getting home for a Saturday night movie. Meeting for drinks after work is not a problem and neither are spur-of-the-moment weekends away.

Then comes the excitement of the first pregnancy: planning the nursery; the incredible moment when that first scan reveals this new little person; the anticipation of the baby's arrival; the anxiety of the labour; the life-changing birth event and the euphoria. It's a real roller-coaster of emotions but *then* the reality sets in …

No more long, leisurely Sunday lie-ins. Gone are the candlelit romantic dinners etc. Now all those unspoken expectations, opinions and previous life experiences begin to surface. Couples slowly realize that the birth of this first, precious and much-loved baby is not as rosy-hued as expected and that, along with the positives, there are also many negatives and enormous adjustments are necessary.

When I ask young couples if anything could have prepared them for the changes parenthood would bring, they all answer, with alacrity, "**No**!" Normally, during our child-less state, we listen to the tales of woe related by parents, observe their discipline mis-takes, shake our heads critically and utter words like, "We will never have children who behave like that," or, "We will be organised and never allow our children to rule our lives." However, the truth is, even if we did a degree in parenting, we would still have to learn by trial and error just how demanding, and all-consuming, parenting can be.

Waking up to reality

I remember clearly the excitement and total delight surrounding the birth of my first child, Catherine. I planned what I would look like as I left the hospital, ensuring that I took my new dress with me (having visions of looking like a member of the Royal Family after the birth). However, what I failed to take into account was the fact that the 'Royals' have dress designers and hair-stylists on tap to hide the flaws and ravages of pregnancy, labour and birth!

I was thoroughly devastated when the zip of my dress was at least 10cm from meet-ing, due to my still-extended midriff, so I therefore had to settle (with feelings of deep disappointment) on my preggie top and elasticised pants that I had worn to the hospital. Thanks to breast engorgement, I also smelt like a greengrocer's shop as a result of cabbage leaves fermenting in my bra. This is a really excellent remedy for that particular malady, although it's not exactly Chanel No. 5! And that was just the first of many shocks. A second major one was the expectation that, because I was so well organised and pre-pared, this tiny 3.5kg baby would be taken home with us and would immediately 'fit in'. Our lives would simply continue as before, with just this little 'added-extra'. That myth exploded after one all-night session with a crying, colicky 5-day-old baby daughter!

I remember feeling enormous anger and resentment towards all the misrepresenta-tive baby adverts for formula, food and toiletries. In every one of them, the baby is peacefully sleeping. The colours are all pastel and hazy and, the biggest con of all, the mothers are slim and well rested, with beatific smiles and expressions that can only come from a full night's sleep and/or a session at the health spa. You never get to see engorged-breasted, black-bags-under-eyes, desperate mothers trying to breastfeed a crying baby whilst stirring a pot of food at the same time!

THE GAINS AND LOSSES

There is no doubt that parenthood is a most incredible, exciting, challenging and reward-ing journey. It provides a wonderful opportunity for personal growth but, in order to adjust and cope, we need to take a good, hard, introspective look at ourselves. We often have to change the way we have reacted previously and review entrenched attitudes and opinions. We suddenly realize that those critically judged parents during our pre-children days were not so bad after all because we are doing exactly the same things! And, hopefully, we then accept the challenge and work at improving our parenting skills.

However, a major problem arises when new parents have expected the arrival of a baby to be an all-positive event. Any hint of negativity is quickly hushed up and new parents (especially mothers) feel guilty to even think a single, negative thought. As mentioned previously though, the fact remains that, as in the laws of science, you cannot have a positive without a negative.

The negatives

When looking at these, it is easier to look at the specifics for the mom, the dad and then the couple.

FOR THE MOTHER

Of course, the arrival of the baby is a very positive event, but it also brings with it a number of losses.

- **The loss of her pre-baby body.** For many women, the body changes bring an enormous loss of self-esteem. This is not helped by media images of celebrity moms wearing tight-fitting jeans when they leave the hospital, and articles on how they are back at the gym within days! During the months after birth, hormones are in a state of flux and turmoil and, as a result, a return to pre-baby fitness and tone can take up to a year.
- **Loss of sleep.** No one can be prepared for the impact of this. After all, sleep deprivation is a well-known form of torture! No wonder new parents appear disoriented and confused – even reading a magazine article can be a challenge.
- **Loss of space and privacy.** As beloved as that new baby is, many mothers feel claustrophobic at times, as if the baby is an extension of herself. Her body does not seem to belong to her anymore. Mothers have said things like, "After giving birth and breast-feeding, I truly feel as if my body is public property. There is just nothing private left."
- **Loss of status, income and peer-support.** As much as they want to be at home with their babies, many first-time moms express the loneliness they feel while adjusting to the loss of income, validation and the peer-group that work provided. There is no salary, there are no days off, no tea breaks or lunch-time shopping and the rewards take a long time coming.

FOR THE FATHER

He feels many of the same stresses and losses. However, as he has not experienced the physical changes his partner has, it is often hard for him to understand the changes in her.

- He often feels the **loss of his previously calm, well-organised and affectionate partner**. He is not Number 1 anymore, as the baby takes all her time and attention.
- **Loss of the intimacy and spontaneity** of their relationship.
- **Loss of freedom and independence** to plan last-minute weekends away etc.
- New fathers often feel **overwhelmed by the feelings of responsibility**, which a baby brings, especially if there is the loss of his partner's salary. He often feels confused and ambivalent. He loves his new baby and may be eager to help and support, yet he is not sure what new-age dads are supposed to do. They need to be empathic and nurturing, yet strong and assertive and able to provide for the family. This is a very ambivalent and confusing role definition.

FOR THE COUPLE

The most striking changes are in their relationship. Aspects which they have never discussed begin to cause stress and tension.

- Even in the most egalitarian relationship, deep-seated **expectations of traditional roles begin to emerge**. Expectations of what women/wives/mothers should do, as well as what is expected of men/husbands/fathers, begin to cause cracks to widen. "But my mother never left us when we were babies," or, "My father made sure my mother never had to worry about money," are statements that can cause disharmony and serious resentment.
- The shift from 'lover' to 'mother' is a huge one, which can be at the root of future relationship breakdown. After childbirth, both parents are usually too shell-shocked to think a single erotic thought! Then sleep deprivation sets in and bed becomes an oasis for sleep – and sleep only. Any romantic expectations are dashed as soon as heads hit pillows. Then, due to less traumatic physical body-changes, **normal male sexual urges begin to return**. However, for his partner, there is still a journey of recovery. She longs for the affection and closeness. She needs to feel wanted and attractive but **usually needs longer to feel sexually alive again**. In the good old days when these issues were never discussed (or admitted), women felt that they were somehow failing (or at fault). I have seen enormous relief in new mothers who share these issues in groups and realize that they are not abnormal or alone. In fact, they are perfectly normal. But this is a vital relationship issue that needs open, understanding communication at a time when emotions are like roller-coasters, and time is all too precious a commodity.
- **Loss of alone time**. Time to connect, share and discuss. The baby becomes the total focus of everything. The baby's feeds become the pivotal aspect of life. Colic, nappies, winds and sleep-patterns become the issue of discussion.

All the above are mentioned in an effort to highlight that, while the arrival of a baby is usually one of the most incredible events in any couple's life, it's also a life-changing and traumatic one. It is positive and maturing yet simultaneously stressful and challenging. Of vital importance is the need to communicate, understand and adjust, as is the case with any major life-change. Positive adaptation does not happen automatically – it takes time and energy. Realising that there could be a need for professional help and support at this stage could be the most important decision a couple can make in order to ensure that the problems do not snowball and cause irreparable damage to their long-term relationship.

A brief word on Post Natal Depression

PND is an extremely serious condition that affects a large percentage of any given female population. It must not be confused with the commonly-experienced 'baby blues' which, as a result of sudden hormone changes, affects most post-natal women on about the third day, at which point a feeling of sadness and weeping can occur at the least provocation.

PND can go undiagnosed for months, as many women feel guilty about their feelings of hopelessness and failure to bond positively with their babies. Many depressed mothers report that, even when they tried to communicate their desperation to those around them, people just didn't understand. They were told to, "Stop being negative, you have this beautiful baby," and, "What about your poor partner? He needs you to snap out of this depression," etc. It is extremely difficult for partners to fully understand what PND really is so they need help and support too. It is, in fact, vital to seek professional help as soon as possible.

These indicators are taken from a pamphlet published by PNDSA (Post Natal Depression South Africa): *The Baby's Fine, How Are You?*
- I feel irritated and confused.
- I cry continuously for no reason.
- I feel exhausted all the time.
- I feel hopeless, unfulfilled and that I cannot cope.
- I worry about my baby all the time.
- I sometimes feel anxious and panicky.
- I blame myself and I feel guilty.
- I don't know who I am anymore.
- I am not interested in anything.

- My sleeping and eating patterns have changed.
- I do not feel bonded to my baby.
- I am not interested in sex.
- I sometimes worry that I may injure my baby or myself.

Most new mothers will be able to answer in the affirmative to at least one or two of these symptoms but, if answers are affirmative to most of the above, professional help should be urgently sought.

The good news is that PND is treatable and that relationships can survive this stress – but not without professional help and ongoing support. Remember that the sooner you recognize the symptoms and get help, the sooner you and your family will function effectively. Speak to your doctor for referral to a qualified counsellor.

The Chinese symbol for crisis has two parts: one symbol which depicts 'a negative event' and another that depicts 'opportunity for personal growth'.

危机

Therefore, any crisis (and the birth of a baby is definitely one of them) involves elements of trauma, but also opportunities for personal growth – and becoming parents most definitely provides plenty of those. As one jaded parent once remarked, "Parenting is like a life sentence!" I do not see it quite so negatively, but it certainly is a life-long commitment and is therefore well worth working on. So, whatever stage of parenting you are at, take a bit of time to explore how well you adjusted to that first hurdle: when baby made three.

"As important as your obligations as a doctor, lawyer or business leader will be ... you are a human being first, and those connections ... with spouses, with children, with friends ... are the most important investments you will ever make. At the end of your life, you will never regret not having passed one more test, not winning one more case, or not closing one more deal. You will regret time not spent with a husband, a child, a friend, or a parent. Our success as a society depends not on what happens in the White House but on what happens inside your house."

Former US First Lady Barbara Bush: A speech to the graduating students of Wellesley College, 1 June 1990

SUMMARY OF CHAPTER 1

- In order to cope with the challenges and demands of the toddler stage, we need to review our adjustment to parenthood.
- The transition from childless couple to couple-with-child is enormous. Gone are the days of spontaneity, privacy, romantic dinners and uninterrupted conversations.
- Although becoming parents is usually positive, exciting and a growth experience, it also comes with many losses and changes.
- For the mother:
  - Loss of pre-baby body (at least for a while).
  - With this, a decline in self-esteem and confidence.
  - Sleep deprivation, which leads to a sense of disorientation and confusion.
  - Loss of space and privacy – that beloved tot seems to be a relentless appendage!
  - Loss of status, income and peer-support. During these early weeks and months it can be very lonely and isolated.
- For the father:
  Many of the same losses as for the mom, but with more emphasis on the following:
  - Loss of his attentive, spontaneous partner, who is now immersed in baby-issues. Many new dads actually feel jealous of the baby.
  - Loss of freedom and independence.
  - Loss of double income, even if temporarily. This often exacerbates the new dad's feelings of responsibility and anxiety.

- For the couple:
  - Deeply ingrained, often unrealistic, expectations regarding the roles of men and women, and dads and moms.
  - Shifts in the woman's role – from 'lover' to 'mother'. Intimacy/sex issues often emerge, and can lead to enormous difficulties.
  - Changes in individual and couple needs – less time for sharing and connections or no time at all.

This all points to the vital need for positive and effective communication. The most precious gift we can give our children is our ability to work through our inevitable problems capably and maturely. It is not *having* problems that causes relationship breakdown, it is our inability to effectively find solutions to them.

2

Can you spoil a baby?

DEVELOPING HEALTHY TRUST

> "Let's be very clear. You **cannot spoil an infant**. Cuddle your infant as much as you want, you won't spoil him. Feed him as often as he's hungry, you won't spoil him. Sing and coo to him as much as you want, you won't spoil him. Pay as much attention to him as often as he cries, you won't spoil him.
>
> The best thing that can happen to your baby, psychologically speaking, is to have as many of his needs gratified and to have as few frustrations as possible. His ego or sense of selfhood is too tender and immature to be able to cope with much frustration now. There will be plenty of time for life to teach him about frustrations when he is older."
>
> Fitzhugh Dodson: *How To Parent*

Many of the problems manifested by toddlers have their roots in ineffective handling of the baby-stage. So let's rewind for just a bit longer before we tackle the 'terrible twos'.

As in my two previous books, I rely heavily on the psychologist, Erik Erikson for an understanding of developmental stages. Therefore a brief repetition is necessary. In his ego psychological theory, Erikson divided the human life spectrum into critical stages of development. At each stage there is a vital task to be worked through as positively as possible. If the critical task is not successfully mastered, there is a negative downside. To illustrate: the task of the adolescent is to develop a sense of identity. However, if they do not manage to achieve this during the turbulent teen years, they will very likely move into the next stage with a sense of identity confusion. This means they will struggle throughout their adult lives with a distorted view of who they are and what their adult roles are.

BACK TO THE BABY-STAGE

Erikson defines this stage as roughly the first year of life, but extending to approximately 18 months, or the emergence from babyhood to toddlerhood.

The vital task of babyhood is to develop a sense of trust. Failure to achieve the sense that important people will be there to meet physical and emotional needs, and that the world is a safe place in which they can grow and develop, will lead to a pervasive sense of distrust. This leads to feelings of insecurity and anxiety, which will be carried over into the toddler stage.

> "The extent to which the infant learns to trust his environment depends mainly on the quality of the mother-child relationship."
>
> "Mothers create a sense of trust in their children by that kind of administration which, in its quality, combines sensitive care of the baby's individual needs and a firm sense of personal trustworthiness within the trusted framework of their culture's lifestyle. This forms the basis in the child for a sense of identity that will later combine a sense of being 'all right', of being oneself and of becoming what other people trust one will become ... Parents must not only have certain ways of guiding by prohibition and permission; they must also be able to represent to the child a deep and almost somatic conviction that there is meaning to what they are doing."
>
> "The successful resolution of the crisis of this stage is the child's acquisition of a healthy trust in the world and herself; faith that her environment will satisfy her need for food, love and attention and also that she is able to satisfy her needs with her cultural environment. Healthy trust is not naive or blind, but is tempered with a degree of distrust which leads to caution."
>
> Erik Erikson: *Personality Theories: from Freud to Frankl*

What does all this theory actually mean?

In a nutshell, that babies are a bundle of needs and demands and that it is critical to their healthy physical and psychological development that these needs are met by mature, capable and caring adults.

Newborn babies have been literally 'ejected' into a world very different from the one they have occupied for nine months. In their previous 'world', they received nourishment on demand, were safely and warmly encased in their mother's amniotic fluid, where they were protected from loud noises and gently rocked when the mother moved. Of course,

research has helped us to understand that the developing foetus is affected by tension and trauma, and that the mother's anxiety and stress is transferred to the baby in-utero. The main point here is the parental need to understand this huge change from the relative safety and tranquillity of the womb, to the realities of the world outside the womb.

Sensory overload

It is an unfortunate aspect of our rushed and stressed 21st century lives, that we find it necessary to catapult these vulnerable and sensitive newborns almost immediately into the bright lights, noise and bustle of supermarkets, malls and restaurants. During a recent visit to my daughter and family in London, one of her friends, a Serbian, had recently given birth to her second child. We were eager to visit, laden with the flowers and gifts one takes to these happy occasions, only to be gently told by her husband that, according to Serbian culture, no one except very close family visits during the first six weeks. The mother and newborn remain quietly at home, being nurtured and fussed over by her husband and close relatives. The baby stays in the quiet, calm nursery, slowly adjusting to life outside the womb and to the immediate family. After six weeks, the doors are gradually opened to friends, and the celebrations can go ahead. By this time most babies are settling into a routine: parents, siblings and baby are bonding and the mother has been able to regain equilibrium.

Of course, many parents of newborns do not have the luxury of six such protected and restful weeks, but it is a model well worth emulating, even if only as far as introducing the baby more gradually and gently to the world outside the womb. Fair enough, many mothers would recoil in horror at the thought of six weeks without coffee at the mall, but try to enjoy such sojourns between feeds, leaving the baby with a childminder. You will feel better after a break, you'll avoid developing 'cabin fever' and the baby will remain in her calm and stress-free environment.

If, as new parents, we fail to put ourselves in the newborn's 'baby socks', expecting him/her to slot into our need for routine and predictability, we will create unnecessary problems for ourselves. There are counsellors, nurses, midwives and doctors who, unfortunately, advise that new parents get their newborns into a rigid routine as soon as possible. To my mind this will only stress the new parents even further as they persevere in attempting to mould the newborn into their expectations of what the baby's routine *should be*, rather than take it calmly and gently and move initially at the baby's pace. It is learning to tune into the baby's early needs, and adjusting accordingly, that will lead to empathic and sensitive parenting … thereby making it easier to establish routines when it is more age-appropriate to do so.

Those were the days!

I well remember the viewpoint that routine should be established from day one. When my first two babies arrived (36 and 34 years ago), the philosophy was very much geared towards four-hourly feeds and 'no picking up unnecessarily, as this will only spoil the baby'. I clearly recall my anguish during those days: three and a half hours after the previous feed, my maternal instinct would be telling me to attend to my screaming five-week-old baby, but I kept hearing that other voice of professional 'wisdom' telling me to train the clearly hungry little mite to wait the four hours! I walked many kilometres in my efforts to get this infant into the routine required by adult needs. The added problem was that I was the type who loved order, structure and predictability so this 'method' suited me very well, but at what a price! In essence, what we had here was a baby who was not learning to trust the world, whose vital infant needs were being ignored, and a mother who was a frazzled, nervous wreck by the time this adored baby was a few weeks old.

Thank goodness for experience and knowledge … by the time the fourth baby came along, it was all about needs and demands and moving at the baby's pace. No clock-watching or walking the streets until the next feed was 'due'. The result: a six-week-old baby who was well on the way to developing a predictable and child-centred routine, with relaxed and connected parents. How wonderful are time, experience and hindsight.

THE BALANCE

So much of parenting is about finding the balance. In that first, vital stage of life it is all about getting to know your baby, learning to anticipate the signal of needs and respond-ing accordingly. Learning the rhythm of their cycles is not easy, but then no new relation-ship is at first. It takes empathy, patience and a very positive mindset, especially as the only way this little bundle of needs can communicate with you initially is via their various levels of crying! The point is this: if you resolutely insist on the need for this tiny person to immediately fit in with your adult lifestyle, you will become extremely stressed and frustrated. This will impact on the baby – they have an inbuilt radar-sensor aimed at your inner feelings and emotional state – and their needs and demands will escalate as they sense your tension and anxiety. The fact is, if you are able to put your life on hold to a certain extent, putting your adult needs on the back burner for the early weeks, you will more easily and readily arrive at a settled and predictable place. There is no doubt that this is very difficult and demanding, but it is all about mindset change and clear, open communication between the adults. Choices that we, as adults, could choose to make.

But what about my needs and demands?

Of course, life has to go on. Older children have to be seen to, chores must be done, partners have to go to work, accounts must be paid, food needs to be purchased (and cooked) …

It must be clearly stated that, when saying that the baby's needs should be of primary importance in order to successfully achieve Erikson's stage of basic trust, it does not mean that the baby will be damaged emotionally when you have other calls on your precious time. The baby may have to yell for a while when you are stirring a pot, getting out of the shower or dealing with another child. The point being made is this: Do not leave the baby to cry simply because someone said you should do this in order to avoid 'spoiling' the baby. You cannot spoil a baby by being available to meet its needs. Unmet needs merely lead to greater and more urgent demands. (Refer back to the quote at the beginning of the chapter.)

Don't feel guilty if you cannot be at his beck and call 24 hours a day. The type of 'distrust' referred to by Erikson, is when there is ongoing, pervasive neglect of infant needs – the type more often seen by child protection social workers.

To summarise: In the words of the baby and toddler expert, Penelope Leach:

"Premature attempts to organise and routinise new babies are intended to diminish the acute stresses of early parenthood but actually increase them. The erratic and inconsistent neonatal behaviours that drive parents crazy will change, and only can be changed, when the infant's physiology has matured and steadied so that he is a settled baby rather than a newborn. The more generously his needs are met in the meanwhile, the sooner that will be, and the generosity pays a long-term dividend too. Newborn babies want nothing that they do not need and therefore do not know how to demand anything more than they need; what they ask for they **do** *need. Having their needs met, readily and kindly throughout the first days and weeks, teaches them that this new world and its caring adults are benevolent and can be trusted, and that trust is the basis of confidence in other people and in self, from infancy to death. Basic trust nourishes self-esteem, nurtures a self of co-operation with others, and guards both when, later on, wants that are not needs must be refused. Even six weeks' total indulgence of a baby's needs will still be paying off when he is six months, six or even sixteen years old. Denied that investment of tender time, denied what they need when and as they need it, newborns suffer and make the parents suffer. Our refusal to recognize and prioritize these earliest human needs creates a vicious circle of infant and parental withdrawal."*

So when do I begin to initiate a bit of boundary-setting?

This is a common question asked by many parents of babies and toddlers. Most new parents today genuinely believe in demand-feeding and keeping the newborn calmly close during the early months. Few seriously discuss the discipline question until their mobile toddler begins to wreak havoc in their well-organised and structured lives. This is when most parents begin to repeat patterns from their own childhood, and those smacks-on-the-hand or on the nappy begin to emerge as the only known methods of behaviour control.

The truth is that the foundations for future effective discipline are laid more-or-less during the middle of the first year, not by initiating smacks or loud verbal admonishments, nor by negatively labelling developmentally normal behaviour.

At around the six-month mark (but there is no absolute or 'magic' age), a rather gradual and gentle process takes place. The urgent new-baby needs begin to evolve slowly but surely into the more predictable needs of the settled baby, and in time, the needs can become demands.

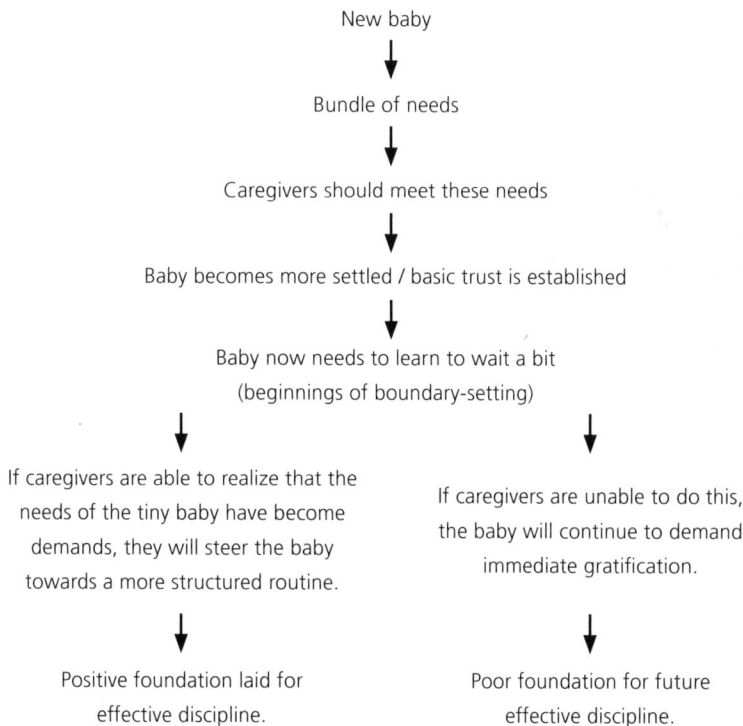

New baby
↓
Bundle of needs
↓
Caregivers should meet these needs
↓
Baby becomes more settled / basic trust is established
↓
Baby now needs to learn to wait a bit
(beginnings of boundary-setting)

↓ | ↓

If caregivers are able to realize that the needs of the tiny baby have become demands, they will steer the baby towards a more structured routine.

If caregivers are unable to do this, the baby will continue to demand immediate gratification.

↓ | ↓

Positive foundation laid for effective discipline.

Poor foundation for future effective discipline.

It becomes very important to tune into the rhythms of the baby's development. By approximately six months old, a baby should be able to tolerate a bit of waiting here and there. This is the time, once the older baby is fed, changed, cuddled and played with, that the parent needs to allow short lessons in frustration tolerance. Put the baby in his chair close to where you are making supper and talk to him calmly and firmly when he begins fussing. This is when age-appropriate boundary-setting begins … you are no longer available at his beck and call twenty-four hours a day.

Many parents make the mistake of continuing the instant-gratification pattern. The baby then expects to have continuous stimulation and immediate attention – a habit which becomes difficult to break. Parents end up exhausted and resentful. The baby/toddler is negatively labelled and then, as if a button has been pressed, "This impossible, demanding child must now be disciplined." Actually, the parents have allowed the demanding behaviour to become entrenched, instead of recognising the need to begin setting some firm, but gentle, boundaries earlier.

There is no doubt that the first steps towards establishing the pattern for future, effective boundary-setting (and therefore positive discipline) lie in the ability, during the first year of your baby's life, to recognize when the very real and urgent needs of the tiny baby become the insistent and determined demands of the older baby. It is up to the parents to be aware of this and to encourage the growing baby to learn that his world won't fall apart and collapse if he has to wait to be picked up, played with, or fed until his caregivers have finished what they are doing. In essence, they learn to wait for just a while for what they want and, by so doing, they learn that the important people in their lives will not abandon them and that they will eventually get what they need.

ROUTINES PROVIDE SECURITY

As much as the newborn needs flexibility, and as baby-centred an approach as possible, the more settled baby responds to the predictability and security of a calm and well-regulated routine. This provides a sense of order and recognizable sameness in their worlds. They feel safely contained within the secure 'walls' of a structured routine. This is not rigid and inflexible, but helps the child to recognize the familiar signs – for example, bath time is followed by quiet playtime, then supper, a cuddle and story time, putting the cuddly toys to bed before she is tucked up in her cot. The baby is gradually being introduced to a world of age-appropriate boundaries, which make future needs for discipline easier to initiate.

In all these ways, the first developmental stage, which primarily involves the development of a sense of basic trust, will have been successfully accomplished. Simultaneously, the firm foundations for boundary-setting will have been laid.

SUMMARY OF CHAPTER 2

- You cannot spoil a newborn baby. Feed on demand, pick up and cuddle, have your baby as close to you as possible. Newborns have recently emerged from a warm, safe, contained environment where all needs are usually met on demand.
- The psychologist, Erik Erikson's theories of personality development are built on the belief that the crucial first challenge for all newborns is to develop a sense of basic trust. And they achieve this by having their needs met by caring, emotionally connected parents. The negative outcome in cases where basic trust is not well established, is for the baby to move into the next developmental stage – the toddler one – with a sense of distrust. It's as if they carry unresolved 'baggage' into their next stage.
- As adults we also have needs and demands on our time and energy. Therefore, we cannot always be instantly available.
- However, never leave a distressed baby to cry for fear of spoiling her. It will only cause unnecessary stress and exacerbate the urgency of the need.
- During these early months, parents *do* need to put their lives on hold. Putting the baby first during the early months will pay enormous dividends later. You will get your identity, your relationship and your lives back.
- The beginnings of boundary setting are laid somewhere around the mid-year mark. When all the basic needs have been met and the baby begins to learn a vital lesson – she cannot always get constant attention but she *will* eventually get what she needs, even if it means a bit of a wait.

3

Emerging from the cocoon

FROM BABYHOOD TO TODDLERHOOD

Ruth Stanford, a colleague of Carl Rogers tells the following story:

The Butterfly

"A compassionate person, seeing a butterfly struggling to free itself from its cocoon, and wanting to help, very gently loosened the filaments to form an opening. The butterfly was freed, emerged from the cocoon, and fluttered about; but could not fly. What the compassionate person did not know was that only through the birth-struggle can the wings grow strong enough for flight. Its shortened life was spent on the ground; it never knew freedom, never really lived."

From the moment the umbilical cord is cut, your baby is no longer physically inseparable from his mother. He becomes a separate being, with his own unique genetic blueprint and separate identity. He is immediately enveloped by the protective containment of caring adults. As discussed in the previous chapter, the newborn is a bundle of instinctive needs and demands, which caregivers should respond to willingly and lovingly. The baby needs this nurturing cocoon. The sooner these needs are met, the sooner the demand can be contained. As the growing baby's needs are met, empathetic parents begin to encourage their infant to learn that her needs will be met, even if she has to wait a while. She is beginning to slowly emerge from the protective casing of her cocoon into the 'real world' of limits and boundaries. During the first year this should be a gradual transition. However, most parents of young babies are guilty of thoughts such as:

"I can't wait until she's three months old – and in a proper routine,"

or

"I wish he was older and more responsive; all he does is eat, sleep and yell!"

I remember falling into this trap. Now, with four grown-up children and the gift of hindsight, I often long for those all-too-fleeting days of their babyhoods. Once they get up and walk and learn to say, "No," they are on their way to freedom and independence.

In fact, babyhood is really over when your infant gets up on two legs and takes those first faltering footsteps. Toddlerhood officially begins at this point. It is also at this point in a child's development that most adults first enter the discipline debate. It is also at this crucial stage when the rocky foundations for future serious discipline problems begin to take root.

THE BABY-TO-TODDLER TRANSITION

Whereas the immobile, crawling or standing baby was relatively easy to control, the curious, rebellious toddler is a very confusing challenge for most new parents. The emerging toddler begins to actively disrupt the order of the home by touching, pulling, climbing and experimenting. Parents, who have usually not given a thought to their views on discipline, begin to react in ineffective and unhelpful ways, concerned that their toddler has emerged from the cocoon and is on his way to becoming an out-of-control brat. It is at this crossroad – from immobile baby to active toddler – that the true meaning of discipline needs to be aired and shared.

Couples need to begin discussing questions such as:

"How were we disciplined?"

"Would that work for today's children?"

"What does smacking actually achieve?"

"Even if we believe in the occasional smack for a toddler, will this still work for an older child and wouldn't it be better to develop more long-term effective methods now?"

In order to answer these questions accurately, we need to take the time to review the toddler issues more fully, beginning with an understanding of the developmental challenges, then moving through issues such as temperament and relationship-building skills, before arriving at the actual business of the true meaning of effective toddler discipline.

This can be graphically depicted as follows:

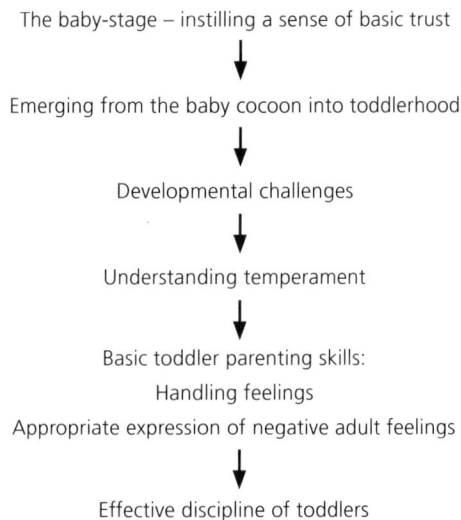

The baby-stage – instilling a sense of basic trust

↓

Emerging from the baby cocoon into toddlerhood

↓

Developmental challenges

↓

Understanding temperament

↓

Basic toddler parenting skills:
Handling feelings
Appropriate expression of negative adult feelings

↓

Effective discipline of toddlers

Developmental challenge of toddlerhood

Many of the parents I have worked with over the years have confided that they knew when their settled, predictable baby was becoming a toddler when she began to yell, "No!" to everything they said. She would look them in the eye, deliberately pull the pot plant out of the soil and then run away screaming, and seemed to prefer pushing all the controls on the TV and DVD player rather than on her Fisher Price musical toy!

The psychologist Fitzhugh Dodson, calls toddlerhood, "The Stage of First Adolescence." He goes on to say:

> *"Second adolescence is a transitional stage between childhood and adulthood. First adolescence is a transitional stage between babyhood and childhood. Both are full of storm and stress. Both involve negotiation and rebellion."*
>
> Fitzhugh Dodson: *How to Parent*

Therefore, when taking this viewpoint into account, it immediately becomes evident that this negative, pot-plant-destroying, yelling little toddler is not being 'naughty' but is actually doing what toddlers are meant to do. This does not mean that parents sit passively by, allowing their emerging toddler to develop into tyrants! However, it should mean that we take the time to understand the toddler's developmental challenges and learn more appropriate management techniques than the knee-jerk reactions of shouting and smacking.

If we learn to understand the underlying purpose of toddler behaviour, we will almost certainly learn more effective methods of boundary-setting in order to contain the unacceptable behaviour. Just as the baby needs to develop a sense of basic trust (which she achieves by having her newborn needs met by capable, caring adults) so too the toddler needs to develop a sense of autonomy and self-identity. She achieves this by rebelling against the controls and restraints put in place by powerful adults.

Bewildered and exhausted parents of toddlers ask this over and over again: "If we have put aside our adult needs and virtually put our lives on hold in order to ensure that we create this important sense of trust in our baby, why on earth does she now emerge from babyhood transformed into this tantrum-throwing, impossible toddler?"

Autonomy vs shame and doubt

According to Erik Erikson, this is the central challenge of toddlerhood. This little person, having emerged from the cocoon of babyhood, now needs to begin expressing his unique individuality and, in so doing, developing the beginnings of independence and separate identity. Fitzhugh Dodson explains it well …

> "Your baby is born with no sense of 'self' or 'I'. It takes him some time to separate out the 'me' from the 'not me' of his environment. This stage of development is the first one in which your youngster acquires a real sense of his own unique selfhood, and one of the things he has to do to establish his own individual sense of identity is to rebel against his parents, and become negativistic. In order for him to define who he is and what he wants to his own satisfaction he has to go through a stage of negating and defying what we want him to do."
>
> Fitzhugh Dodson: How to Parent

So, is it normal behaviour for toddlers to:
- say "no" to anything and everything?
- have temper tantrums?
- resist orders and instructions?
- rebel against absolute orders?
- regress – be able to do something one day and not the next?
- behave aggressively and irrationally?
- be totally egocentric and unable to share?

The answers to all of the above is a loud and clear, "Yes!" In order to assert their independence and individuality, this is exactly what toddlers do, which is why this is such a challenging and exhausting stage for the parents of toddlers. It is a matter of understanding that these annoying behaviours are not intentional naughtiness, but do need to be contained and effectively channelled.

The possible pitfalls

As stated earlier, this is a crucial stage for the outcome of effective discipline. Why? Because the very necessary mini-rebellions of the toddler-stage are often in direct conflict with parental expectations and standards. The parents need to have a well-behaved, socially-acceptable child, one who eats nicely, goes to sleep on cue, is quietly and quickly potty-trained, shares her toys at Toddler Group and (especially) one whose first identifiable phrase is: "Thank you, Granny"!

Parents then feel anxious and pressured when their beautiful, adored, happy pre-toddler behaves anything like this! She spits out her food; gets out of bed twenty times before finally falling asleep after a parental 'meltdown'; wets her pants after adamantly refusing to sit on the potty; her first word is, "No!" her first phrase is, "Don't like you, Granny," and, to cap it all, she hits the other toddlers at playgroup if they so much as dare to look at a toy ear-marked by her for sole ownership!

Well-meaning grandparents then utter words like:

"You'd better nip this in the bud. Your uncle Jeremy was just like this at two, and look at him now." (And you know that Uncle Jeremy is having enforced anger management therapy as a condition of keeping his job)

or,

"All he needs is a good smack in order to learn who is boss", though you have resolutely decided not to use physical punishment as an effective method of discipline.

But the doubt begins to creep in ... Maybe nothing else will work? Perhaps a toddler like this does need to be smacked or, "I really didn't want to smack and yell, but this child just drives me mad and I can't help myself!"

We will work towards how to effectively and assertively manage the problem behaviours via positive management skills. At this point, it is sufficient to stress the fact that these infuriating and exhausting behaviours are 'normal' for a child at this age and stage of development.

This does not mean that we sit idly by and ignore the tyrannical behaviour, but it does mean that, before reacting with appropriate containment methods, we should have internalised into our belief system that the negativistic, anti-social behaviours are all part-and-parcel of the toddler developmental challenges.

How else does a little person express his feelings to these adults who are trying to control his every action, when his inner 'voice' is saying something like:

"You are you – a separate person – and you need to let these powerful dictators around you know that you can resist their unrealistic expectations and absolute orders by becoming just as adamant."

Toddlers may not yet have the verbal skills, or the necessary levels of emotional intelligence to get this message across, but they certainly know how to do it. They very quickly learn the power of yelling, kicking, screaming and refusing to co-operate, thereby catapulting these determined and controlling adults into a downward-spiralling power struggle. It is a terrible state of affairs when a tiny, furious two-year-old can reduce a 30-year-old into a just-as-furious, spluttering, incoherent, out-of-control state of anger.

We have a journey to travel from this point; a journey that will touch on all the relevant insights and skills, with the ultimate goal being one where the adult has the ability to remain calmly and firmly containing. The first part of that journey is to thoroughly embrace this crucial fact of toddler behaviour.

The main challenge, once the basic trust of infancy is accomplished, is to understand that the toddler's developmental challenge should be allowed to develop a sense of autonomy/independence, and he does this by challenging the controls and obstacles put in his way by the adults in his life.

The possible problems if this stage is not well handled

As outlined previously, Erikson's stages include a downside: when the challenges are not positively achieved, there is a negative outcome. If the baby does not have its needs met, a sense of mistrust will predominate and there will be a feeling that caregivers and, by implication also, the world in general, cannot be trusted. In the case of the toddler's need to develop autonomy, over-control (and therefore, usually overly-harsh and age-inappropriate discipline) will stultify the toddler's innate need to develop a sense of 'me-ness'. There can be many negative outcomes of this unfortunate situation:

- The 'good' toddler then quickly learns that it is better to toe the adult line, at the expense of that essential first step towards an independent identity and early assertiveness skills.

- The toddler's immature and unskilled attempts at self-assertion are met with adult aggression and over-control, which serve only to exacerbate the aggressive toddler behaviour. A very long-term cycle of reinforcing aggression is set in motion. The toddler is then clearly denied the opportunity to develop more mature and skilful methods of expressing autonomy.

- Toddlers develop a pervasive sense of what Erikson terms "shame and doubt". When everything they attempt, in order to assert their autonomy, is met with punitive control and negative labelling, their developing self-concept is negatively distorted and they begin to view themselves as bad, naughty, incapable etc. When we feel bad about ourselves, we are more likely to behave badly, so the cycle for future, ongoing, discipline problems can take hold simply because adults view the normal negative behaviour of toddlers in an unfortunately unrealistic light.

To quote Erikson again:

> "This stage, therefore, becomes decisive for the ratio of love and hate, co-operation and wilfulness, freedom of self-expression and its suppression. From a sense of self-control without loss of self-esteem comes a lasting sense of good will and pride; from a sense of loss of self-control and of foreign over-control comes a lasting propensity for doubt and shame."
>
> Personality Theories: from Freud to Frankl

SUMMARY OF CHAPTER 3

- The onset of the stage of toddlerhood is not so much age-dependent as it is behaviourally defined. Simply put, it begins when the baby takes those first, shaky, 'toddling' steps. However, it is more recognizable by the well-known behaviours that typify the 'terrible twos': the 'Nos', the tantrums and the refusal to cooperate with adult standards and expectations.
- The baby is emerging from the more predictable, nurturing and contained 'cocoon' of the early months.
- In order to develop a healthy psychological sense of identity and independence, the toddler needs to fight restrictions and over-control. This is the only way in which they can learn to strengthen their immature 'wings' in order to 'fly' towards future freedom and separateness.
- Erik Erikson calls this stage, autonomy vs shame and doubt. In other words, the adults in the toddler's life need to understand how to help the child achieve full independence. Mostly, this is via an internalisation of the meaning of effective discipline.
- Failure to achieve this (usually due to unrealistic expectations, over-harsh and outdated views on discipline and negative labelling) can lead to serious self-esteem issues and to downward-spiralling parent-child relationships, with the strong possibility of ongoing serious discipline problems.

4

What about the parents?

RECLAIMING YOUR SANITY

> *"Maintaining understanding requires frequent and effective communication; couples need to check in, be proactive, and invest in their parenting partnership. Unfortunately, what often happens post-baby is disengagement, which leaves each partner feeling alone and misunderstood."*
>
> Alison Osborne: *The Post Baby Conversation: What new parents say to each other*

Before continuing along the rough road of effectively establishing boundaries for toddlers, we need to pause for a few moments and concentrate on adult issues. As the baby evolves into a mobile, talkative, curious and self-willed toddler, her parents need to reconnect and recommit to their relationship. The early weeks and months of baby-hood are all-consuming and exhausting. Many parents of toddlers feel as if they too are emerging from a cocoon (although some call it a dark tunnel or even a complete fog!). The urgent needs of their tiny baby begin to feel less demanding. Establishment of a predictable routine makes it possible to plan outings and to invite friends for dinner and Sunday lunches again. It is possible to leave the toddler with a trusted babysitter … in short, there *is* life after babies!

You may be wondering why I am repeating the issues already mentioned in Chapter 1. I cannot emphasize strongly enough how important it is to take stock of your adult relationships at this transitional stage. In fact, if possible, this would be printed in bright, flashing, neon lights!

> The best gift you can give your toddler is to ensure that you look after your personal growth and identity issues, and nurture your adult relationships.

THE PROBLEMS AND PITFALLS

Just as the adjustment to parenting is a complicated process, so too is the process of moving from the stage of the total dependency of babyhood to the challenges of the toddler stage. It is so easy to allow unresolved problems and escalating resentments to become an excuse to remain over-involved with the baby, and then the toddler, at the expense of your relationship with your partner. I have traced the beginnings of the disintegration of many relationships to problems that emerged after the arrival of the first baby (and which were sadly 'brushed under the carpet') only to escalate and gather momentum later, until the chasm between the parties becomes too enormous for effective bridge-building. Below are some of the reasons for this all-too-frequent outcome:

Prolonged over-involvement

Newborns need around-the-clock attention. Many parents, especially mothers, find it very difficult to know when this dependence needs to move towards a gentle separation, which leads to less dependence and psychologically healthy individuation. It becomes emotionally painful to leave the baby or to trust anyone else to care adequately for her. Even the child's other parent is not fully trusted!

Identity enmeshment

Initially the newborn is an integral part of the primary caregiver (usually the mother). For some, the baby becomes an important confirmation of their self-worth and their identity becomes totally enmeshed with their baby. While it is one of the most satisfactory ways of feeling fulfilled – as an individual and as a family – the birth of a baby should not become the total manifestation of one's worth as a human being. What can begin to take shape is an unhealthy family system whereby the infant becomes the total focus of a parent's life, at the expense of the ongoing need to maintain a positive connection with an adult partner.

Healthy family system

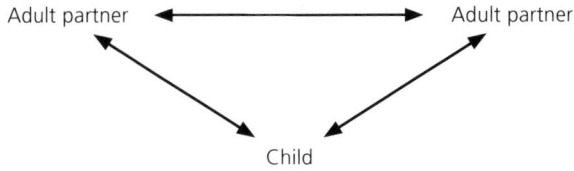

Adult partner ⟷ Adult partner

Child

Unhealthy family system

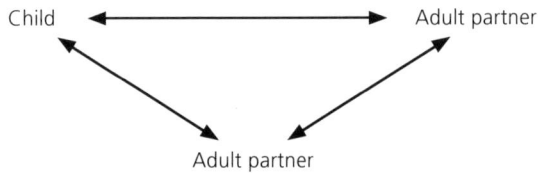

Child ⟷ Adult partner

Adult partner

When this type of adult-toddler enmeshment exists, the disconnected adult feels isolated and resentful. This inevitably leads to escalating tension and conflict, and almost certain eventual separation. It also impacts negatively on the toddler's healthy emotional development and makes effective parenting and discipline very challenging.

It masks other problems

Immersing oneself in the needs of a baby, and the demands of a toddler, can also be a means by which deeper issues are masked. Many a troubled person has told me in counselling sessions that they had a baby as a means of repairing problems in their relationships, or as a result of pressure from a partner. The baby then becomes all consuming and pivotal in their lives and an 'excuse' to pull away from the troubled relationship. This is an intolerable burden to place on a child and the resulting dysfunctional relationship will almost certainly exacerbate the problems rather than alleviate them.

Rather than achieving any attempt at suppressing or avoiding unresolved frustrations and disappointments, the stress that the adjustment to parenthood involves will often act as a trigger, whereby the suppressed feelings and issues will only become magnified. The baby/toddler then becomes an excuse: a means to avoid dealing directly with any interpersonal difficulties. Communication becomes superficial, intimacy is avoided and time alone is dreaded. All because of the needs and demands of this little person, who would infinitely prefer (in the long run, anyway), that his parents enjoy a fulfilling and mutually-rewarding adult relationship, as this provides the best launch pad for him to begin his own long journey towards eventual independence and healthy psychological separation from parents.

The guilt trap

I once read a book that made a comment along the lines that guilt is such a feminine emotion, it should be written in pink ink! I have often thought of it since then and find that it is very true. It seems to be tied up with those myths and entrenched opinions of the good old days … *Good mothers devote themselves to their children. They are self-sacrificing and put the needs of their families first,* etc.

So, after those early days when it is essential to put the needs of their babies first, many mothers find it difficult to reclaim their identities and, sadly, some never do. Then, after years of self-denial and identity-suppression, those over-protected and indulged children leave home (as they should), leaving mothers feeling abandoned and lonely – with identity confusion and the whole empty-nest syndrome firmly in place. Thereafter, the mothers spend the rest of their lives burdening their children with guilt for abandoning them after they had put everything into raising them: a serious case of unhealthy guilt.

It is interesting to note that, as a rule, fathers seem to escape the guilt trap. (Perhaps because the moms absorb enough for both of them! Possibly, if the moms let go of some of it, the dads would take on a healthy dose.) Fathers miss PTA meetings, ballet concerts, pre-school birthday parties and parenting talks, usually with comments like, "Well, I have to work and her mom is so good at it. She loves all the concerts and parties." Dads also don't feel a vestige of guilt when they take off afternoons to play 'work-related golf' or to watch rugby with their mates. So … moms, you need to become more assertive: push those debilitating and insidiously destructive guilt twinges into the sidelines of your consciousness, where they will hopefully wilt and slowly die. It is therefore vital to avoid the guilt trap from the beginning.

STEPS TOWARDS HEALTHY SEPARATION

This may not be easy, especially if you already have a baby or toddler and recognize your-self in some (if not all) of the above points. However, it is important to take these steps to ensure that your family doesn't suffer later as a result of your inability to let go.

You are not infallible

I remember well those early days, when I truly felt that no-one else would ever be able to understand my baby or be capable of caring for her as well as I could – not even my very supportive and involved husband. This became a double-edged sword: I was exhausted and yearning for time alone (even if just to have baby-free bath time or a ten minute magazine session on my bed) yet some primal inner 'voice' was telling me that no-one else could be trusted, not even for these few minutes.

Tell yourself, as early as possible, that others can be trusted and that you are not indispensable. Try delegating as soon as possible. You don't need to leave your three-day-old baby while you go off to Mauritius for a long weekend, but allow someone else to help out while you relax in an aromatherapy bath for fifteen wonderful, baby-free minutes.

Trust your partner with child-care tasks

I have had many a confused new father share with me a situation such as this:

> "My wife is utterly exhausted and accuses me of not understanding what it's like for her to be alone with the baby all day. But when I do try to help, she stands over me and criticizes everything I do: the nappy is too loose; the bib is too tight; I am holding the bottle wrong. Nothing is ever right so I just stop trying."

Encourage your partner to become actively involved, as this will positively influence your co-parenting skills and will be enormously beneficial for your positive communication and connectedness. So what if the nappy is too loose or too tight? He will soon become just as adept at it as you are. Remember that it wasn't too long ago that it wasn't fitting for 'real men' to have anything to do with either the nursery or anything relating to babies. New-age fathers have come a long way since those days, but they still need a lot of encouragement, positive reinforcement and a measure of gentle prodding.

Take small steps

As the rather clichéd saying goes: *Every journey starts with the first step.* The parenting journey is no exception. As the baby grows towards toddlerhood, begin to take the gradual steps that will lead you towards a healthy balance between the inevitable needs of your young child, the nurturing and continuous development of your own needs and identity, and those of your relationship with your partner.

At the beginning, the very thought of getting a babysitter and getting ready to go out is daunting enough to avoid for as long as possible. I vividly remember our 2nd wedding anniversary: a six-week-old baby, mother-in-law roped in to come and baby-sit and dinner booked at a nearby restaurant. The baby was colicky, I was a bundle of nerves and my husband and I were too exhausted to talk, let alone eat. We looked at each other, had a drink and dragged ourselves back home after an hour! However, at least we made the effort. Needless to say, we mutually agreed not to repeat this for a while but you *should* try and make the effort during that first year. Remember to keep the balance.

Make time to share

Right from the beginning (even if it is only five minutes over a cup of tea before you fall into bed to grab as much sleep as the baby allows), make a point of sharing and listening. Remember the illustration regarding the Chinese symbols for 'crisis' and see this as also being an opportunity for personal growth. By staying connected, even if somewhat precariously at first, you will avoid misunderstandings and resentment. Sadly, it is so easy to allow the distance to grow but it is also relatively easy to try to take those small steps towards keeping the communication open.

EMERGING FROM YOUR COCOON

As your baby becomes a toddler, you too will feel yourself emerging from the cocoon that has totally encapsulated you and your baby during the first year of her life. Your ability to take back some of your spontaneity and freedom, and to prioritize the maintenance of your relationship with your partner, will provide an essential foundation for the challenges that lie ahead during the toddler stage. Your resilience, positive self-esteem and clear boundaries in your own life will be every bit as important for your toddler as your ability to fully understand the developmental challenges he is experiencing. When those inevitable twinges of guilt appear to fill you with doubt, remember the long-term effects of the guilt trap, especially for mothers. It is healthy for the whole family's emotional well-being to take time out to:

• relax at the hair salon or health spa.
• enjoy a coffee break at the mall with friends (without taking the toddler).
• go to the movies, followed by dinner.
• take a moonlight stroll on the beach with your partner.
• arrange for a night away at a romantic destination.

Of course, you obviously need to ensure that you have a trustworthy carer!

Now that I have given a brief overview of the important issues that lead up to the toddler stage, including a discussion of the developmental challenges that the toddler has to work through, I can proceed with this little person's journey: moving from babyhood to childhood via the tempestuous toddler stage, or the terrible twos!

....

SUMMARY OF CHAPTER 4

• As parents emerge from the foggy cocoon of their baby's first year, it is really important to reconnect as a couple before regaining their strength to tackle the toddler stage.
• Some of the problems and pitfalls:
  – The prolonged, over-involvement with the all-consuming needs of the baby, and reluctance to let go and trust others – even the other parent.
  – Identity enmeshment – failure to begin the very necessary process of separation.
  – Allowing the needs of the baby to mask other problems in the relationship.
  – Falling into the guilt trap. Feeling bad about reclaiming adult relationships and identity.
• Steps towards healthy separation
  – Realise that you are not infallible.
  – Encourage your partner to become actively involved.
  – Take small steps.
  – Make time to share and connect.

In *The post-baby conversation*, Alison Osborne, uses the following quote by John Gottman, a professor of psychology: *"A lasting marriage results from a couple's ability to resolve the conflicts that are inevitable in any relationship … no matter what problem-solving style a partnership follows, the couple must have at least five times as many positive as negative moments together if the relationship is to be stable. Negativity builds as laughter and validation cease and criticism and pain build up."*

5

Determinants of toddler behaviour

SOME ARE JUST BORN MORE CHALLENGING

The scene is now set for a thorough perusal of all the issues relevant to this most important of developmental stages – toddlerhood. As stated in my book, *Children Need Boundaries*, all behaviour is purposeful. We do things for a reason (although as we get older, more and more of our behaviour is subconscious) and toddlers are no exception. They behave as they do for a reason, as inexplicable as much of their behaviour may seem to the adults in their lives.

In Chapter 3 I gave you some input into, arguably, the most important determinant of toddler behaviour – their developmental stage. To recap briefly:

Toddlers need to rebel, to become controlling and negative, all in order to establish their sense of autonomy and separate identity. They are doing what their inner developmental 'clock' is telling them to do. The challenge for parents is to learn to manage the unacceptable behaviour as calmly and effectively as possible.

THE TEMPERAMENT

The other important determinant of toddler behaviour is that of their genetically ordained temperaments. At conception, the genetic raw material is encoded in strands of DNA, which determines so much of each individual person.

> "Each child has his or her own natural, inborn temperament which shapes their behaviour from a very young age ... Although parents and the greater environment influence temperament and interplay with it they are not able to change this aspect of children's personalities. The task of parents is to help their children manage their sometimes difficult temperament traits. For example, children need to learn how to contain their very intense emotions. They need to learn how to pay attention for longer periods as they progress through school."
>
> Positive Parenting Manual Skills for South African Parents

The emphasis must be on the very important fact that there is definitely a core, pre-ordained, genetic link to temperament. Some children are amenable and reasonable from a very young age. Others are stubborn and challenging. The key to whether the negative behaviour will become reinforced and escalate, or be effectively channelled so that the positive side of the behaviour is encouraged, depends almost entirely on the way in which the parents manage the behaviour via their parenting skills.

> **Hence the vital importance of taking time to learn how to be the best possible manager of your unique child's temperament.**

But what exactly is temperament?

In his book, *The Difficult Child*, Stanley Turecki has the following excellent explanation:

> *"Temperament is the natural, inborn style of behaviour of each individual. It's the **how** of behaviour, not the **why**. It should not be confused with motivation. The question is not 'Why does he behave a certain way if he doesn't get a cookie' but rather, 'When he doesn't get a cookie, **how** does he express his displeasure? Does he pout? Does he whine and complain? Or does he kick and scream?' This style of behaviour is innate and is not produced by the environment. The environment – and your behaviour as a parent – can influence temperament and interplay with it, but it is not the cause of temperamental characteristics."*

At this point it is necessary to accept that, just as the developmental stage affects behaviour, so too does temperament.

The double whammy

If you have been blessed with a determined, strong-willed and stubborn toddler – all traits that are linked to the core temperament – and he is well and truly in the developmental stage of the 'terrible twos', you could have a real 'double whammy' on your hands. Toddlers, as we have discussed, are meant to be negative, egocentric, irrational and stubborn. If you have one who also possesses a challenging temperament, all the above traits will probably be magnified a hundredfold.

Avoid the pitfalls of negative labelling

Right from birth, parents and caregivers fall into the trap of negative labelling. A newborn baby is labelled 'good' and 'easy' if she sleeps between feeds, shows no signs of colic and sleeps through the night from an early age. Does this then make a colicky, high-need baby 'naughty'? Does it mean that the amenable, calm and easy-to-discipline toddler is a model child and the more demanding, volatile and defiant one is a future delinquent?

This is the insidiously damaging effect of early childhood labelling – those labels stick and become self-fulfilling prophecies. The good, easy baby earns praise and approval that, in turn, leads to co-operative, rewarding behaviour, and the positive labels are more likely to continue into toddlerhood. On the other hand, the high-need baby is more likely to be negatively labelled and to become a more difficult and challenging toddler, with the resultant escalating negative labels. The trouble with self-fulfilling prophecies is that children learn to live up to their labels.

It seems to work like this: If a toddler is told often enough that he is bad, naughty, a bully, driving his parents crazy and causing them to have a nervous breakdown, he will internalise these negative messages and behave accordingly. He begins to tell himself, "Well, if I am so bad, then I may as well be really good at it!" And he proves that this is very possible, although of course this is mostly at a subconscious level. Some children are just born difficult, which makes positive labelling very challenging but, in order to manage the behaviour as effectively as possible, it is crucial to look for the positives in the child's temperament. Just as in science you won't find a negative without a positive, an action without a reaction, so it is with temperament qualities.

> **Difficult** can be seen as **challenging**
> **Stubborn** can be seen as **determined**
> **Aggressive** can be seen as **assertive**
> **Defiant** can be seen as **strong-willed**
> **Irrational** can be seen as **emotional**

By working hard to see the positive qualities on the other side of the negatives, it becomes easier to retain an open mind and help the toddler to see that the behavioural manifestations of the negative traits, positively managed, can be channelled into positive and acceptable behaviours. A well-managed, aggressively inclined toddler will almost certainly develop into an assertive older child. In short:

> Beware the labelling trap. If toddlers are negatively labelled for behaviours that are developmentally normal, chances are the behaviours will escalate and become entrenched.

This does not in any way mean that the unacceptable behaviour is condoned, with the parent blandly turning a blind eye to the aggressive, anti-social toddler behaviour and adopting the attitude that *he is just being a toddler and he is just like me, stubborn and strong-willed.* Not at all! Capable, informed parents will take appropriate action via the necessary boundaries they will put in place, but the effective discipline of their very determined toddler will be made easier if they have internalised a more positive attitude towards the underlying determinants of the behaviour. As a prerequisite for coping effectively with the challenges of toddlerhood, this cannot be stressed enough.

OTHER DETERMINANTS OF BEHAVIOUR

Of course, the list of what causes behaviour – both positive and negative – is very long: hunger, thirst, fatigue, over-stimulation, over-harsh discipline, unrealistic expectations, parental conflict and tension. I am concentrating here on the determinants that are difficult to change, as in the case of temperament and development stage.

The Positive Parenting Manual is very helpful when it comes to describing the other, less powerful, determinants:

Position in the family

"Children's positions in the family significantly affect their experiences and thus their perceptions of the world. We refer here to the birth order which provides each with unique experiences, as well as to the roles that children unconsciously adopt within the family in an attempt to meet their emotional and social needs.

The oldest child starts off being an only and often treasured child who, very early in life, has to manage the trauma of giving up the throne and sharing his parent's affection and attention with the second born. First-born children often tend to feel the need to be responsible, in control, caring and pressurised to meet their parents' expectations.

Second children often have to cope with the first child's resentment at having to share their parent's affection with them. They can become the victims of aggressive attacks and have to learn to defend themselves. They often feel a certain security at having an older protector but resent having to do with 'hand-me-downs'. They may feel unfairly compared to the older child. Although they have no expectation of exclusive attention from parents and are able to share more easily, they also need time alone with their parents.

The middle child often experiences feeling 'squeezed out' and unspecial. They are neither the responsible child nor the special 'baby'. They may feel jealous of both the older and the younger child and feel strongly about fairness and issues of right and wrong. They often tend to just get on with life and are able to pair off with either the younger or older child.

The youngest or last child presents the last chance experienced parents have of 'doing it right'. In many ways it's an ideal position in the family as it provides all the advantages of years of trial and error learning. Youngest children tend to be less pressured, more charming and confident. They can be overindulged and overprotected and often express feelings of not being allowed to grow up, not taken seriously nor respected and not given enough responsibilities.

Where there is only one child in a family, such only-children do not have to share or fight for their rights but may regret the lack of sibling companionship. Being alone they have all the advantages of not having to share the available financial and emotional resources. They do, however, often feel pressured to succeed by their parents who may have unrealistic expectations about children their age. With their parent's attention solely focused on them they often feel a strong need to establish some privacy and a space for themselves in the home."

Gender

Traditionally, little boys did not play with dolls and were allowed to be more aggressive, while little girls would help mom with the cooking and were expected to be kind and gentle. Even in today's more egalitarian society, where these roles are less strictly entrenched, parents still have different expectations for their sons and daughters. Role-definition is very deeply embedded in our subconscious psyche. Parents may overtly declare that they are fully accepting of their three-year-old son's penchant for wearing a fairy dress and playing with his sister's Barbie dolls, but there is a measure of deep-seated unease nonetheless. The *Positive Parenting Manual* goes on to say:

"Most cultures expect women to be more nurturing and emotionally expressive than men, and men to be more aggressive and ambitious than women."

The main issue here is that we need to give clear messages to our children, to understand that boys and girls are different (in more ways than the obvious ones) and realize that their gender will be a determinant of their behaviour. In short, while encouraging them to feel relaxed about who and how they are while they are toddlers, we need not go overboard in our attempts to encourage girls to be more like boys and vice versa.

Life experiences

"Every child has unique life experiences, some of which may leave lasting impressions and affect their understanding of the world, resulting behaviour, and future management of their lives. These include problematic situations such as moving home, divorce, the loss of a parent through death, sickness and hospitalisation, physical, sexual or emotional abuse, school failure, poverty, social turmoil, learning difficulties, or mental handicap. Some positive life experiences include a close and reliable relationship and attachment with parental figures; a sufficiently supportive and encouraging home and school environment; successful peer relationships, some successes at school and extramurally."
Positive Parenting Manual: Skills for South African Parents

The issue to bear in mind here is that 'stuff happens'. Toddlers get ill and have to be hospitalised. Grandparents die, as do pets. Parents separate and divorce, or are retrenched. Families move. Violence and crime impact on family security. Most of these traumatic life events impact directly on families and therefore also on the children concerned. These experiences then impact *very directly* on behaviour. As in the examples of developmental stages (temperament, gender and position in the family), life experiences need to be borne in mind when disciplining effectively, but should never be an excuse for unacceptable behaviour. It is very important to be able to decode toddler behaviour.

"I realize she is feeling insecure because we just moved house and her dad is working overseas for two months, but she still should not be allowed to bite and scratch her four-year-old sister."

So ... we need to have a clear grasp of the underlying factors that determine toddler behaviour but, nonetheless, while being empathetic to the probable reasons we still need to put very clear, consistent and age-appropriate boundaries in place.

THE ADULT REACTION DETERMINES FUTURE BEHAVIOUR

While the determinants listed are difficult to change, what we *can* change, as mature and capable parents, is our attitude, perception and reaction to our toddler's behaviour. And here I need to once again repeat my favourite quote from Stephen Covey's, *The 7 Habits of Highly Successful Families*:

"*Between stimulus and response there is a space. In that space lies our freedom and power to choose our response. In our response lies our growth and our happiness.*"

STIMULUS ⟶ **FREEDOM TO CHOOSE** ⟶ RESPONSE

Stephen Covey also uses the powerful image of a console to illustrate the point that, as parents of exasperating, irritating, infuriating children, *we must be in control of our pause buttons*.

In the case of toddlers especially, who are in a very negative stage of development, adults need to have control of that vital **pause** button. They will push our **play** button as hard, and determinedly, as they know how, so we need to have internalised the belief that *he may push and push the boundaries, but I am the mature adult and will not allow my play button to be pushed. I am calmly but firmly in control of that vital pause button!*

Too many exhausted parents, especially those of toddlers, keep repeating lame and defeatist mantras. For example:

"She made me shout at her."

"He was asking for a smack."

"My toddler forces me to lie with her until she's asleep."

"My wife and I haven't had a night out in three years. Kayla throws a fit if we leave her with anyone else."

What has happened here? The normal determinants of behaviour have allowed frazzled parents to hand power over to their tyrannical toddlers. This is clearly not a healthy recipe for future effective discipline.

....

SUMMARY OF CHAPTER 5

- Chapter 3 dealt with the developmental challenges of toddlerhood. There is no doubt that the characteristic behaviour of this stage plays a very dominant role as a determinant of behaviour.
- The second important determinant is the child's genetically programmed temperament – that component of the child's unique make-up that plays an ongoing role in behavioural manifestations.
- Some children are born with the predisposition to be easy and amenable. They are given positive labels that lead to an ongoing propensity to be co-operative and relatively easy to discipline.
- Others are born with more stubborn, strong-willed and aggressive tendencies. They are labelled more critically and negatively, which will lead to a self-fulfilling prophecy. They will be inclined to behave according to their labels.
- Adults ought to be aware of the long-term ill effects of these negative labels and try to remember that there are always two sides to the same coin. Even though the negative quality is undeniably present, being able to remember that a positive label is lurking somewhere on the other side of that proverbial coin will help to avoid the entrenchment of a negative attitude.
- Other determinants of behaviour are: the *position* in the family, the *gender* and life *experiences*.
- While many determinants cannot be changed, parents are challenged to work on internalising more effective attitudes and reactions.
- Capable, confident and skilled parents believe that they are in charge of their **pause** button, and they make choices regarding their responses to the child's behaviour.
- Accepting that certain underlying factors are determinants of toddler behaviour does not mean that unacceptable behaviour is ignored. It means that a more positive and realistic mindset will ensure that the discipline/boundary-setting is more effective.

6

Toddler feelings

THE CORNERSTONE OF FUTURE EMOTIONAL INTELLIGENCE

"To raise psychologically healthy children, with a strong self-concept, parents should allow children to express their feelings. The actual facts, unfortunately, are otherwise. Most parents do not allow children to express their feelings freely."

"One of the basic things that adults with psychological problems learn through psychotherapy is how to express their feelings adequately. But if we teach them to express their feelings adequately when they are little children, they will have good mental health when they become adults."

Fitzhugh Dodson: *How to Parent*

Over the years I have observed a direct link between healthy adult mental health and high levels of emotional intelligence. And what is the core issue in emotional intelligence? The ability to be in touch with your feelings and knowing how to express them appropriately. I believe strongly that it is at the toddler stage that most future emotional problems are incubated. Why? Because toddlers are glibly 'punished' for their feelings. Parents may react vehemently to this statement with retorts like, "But I'm not punishing his feelings, I'm limiting his bad behaviour." Fair enough, but how do two-year-olds, just beginning to make coherent sentences, express how they are feeling? Usually by behaving badly. In other words, the typical toddler behaviour, which is often the outward manifestation of an inner state they do not yet have the ability to express, is dealt with over-severely and, by this inappropriate reaction, they are not being encouraged to learn a vital life-skill.

> **Feelings are always acceptable, but sometimes, the behaviour we choose to express these feelings, is not.**

BACK TO BASICS

How do we get to know what we are feeling? As parents of toddlers this is a very important question. Take the time to listen to parents of babies. Usually, they have no problem labelling objects. "Look at the pretty butterfly," they will say happily to their three-month-old. "That's a big, blue balloon," they say to their four-month-old at his cousin's birthday party. So this is how babies begin to identify butterflies and balloons, and before long, he is copying and trying out the labels too.

So why is it so much harder to label a baby's feelings? Many a parent has answered me with: "How do I know how she is feeling?" My reply is, "Because we develop an empathic connection and learn to decode body language." To quote from Dorothy Corkille Briggs:

> *"Empathy is being understood from your point of view. It means that another person enters your world and proves that he understands your feelings by reflecting back your message. He temporarily sets aside his world to be 'with' you in all the subtleties of meaning that a particular situation has for you. As Carl Rogers has pointed out, the empathic person is with you, not to agree or disagree, but rather to understand without judgment."*

To further emphasize the vital importance of empathy, she says:

> *"Empathy gets love across … it follows warm closeness – intimacy; it wipes out loneliness. Just as empathy draws a child closer to you, it moves you closer to him. For when you walk in another's shoes, when you truly get a feel for his viewpoint, suddenly something happens; his behaviour makes sense."*
>
> *Your Child's Self-Esteem*

So, when you are changing your baby's nappy, he's yelling blue murder and you can see he is *not* happy – in fact, he is as mad as a snake – you say to him:

"I can see you hate this – it makes you very angry."

And when he pulls a face and spits out his pureed butternut, why not try saying:
    "Gosh, you really didn't like that."

When he starts crying in his cot as soon as he's just woken up:
    "I think you're feeling very lonely and want someone to come and pick you up."

A most vital skill

Learning to decode behaviour and suggesting labels for feelings are, I believe, *the* most vital parenting skill to ensure that your child becomes an emotionally intelligent child/ teenager in the future.

Just as your toddler will begin to know the labels for objects, she will also begin to know the labels for her feelings. Labelling feelings takes more verbal maturity than labelling items, so parents need to persevere patiently during the toddler stage, when toddlers experience immensely strong feelings but do not yet have the maturity to express them. Due to this lack of verbal maturity, they have no outlet other than their typically negative toddler behaviour.

Put yourself in your toddler's shoes for just a few minutes: You are playing happily with the sprinkler in the garden, making a lovely, muddy mess. Suddenly, your mom comes running out, very stressed and agitated because it's time to go to granny for tea and she didn't realize how late it is. She grabs the hose, turns off the water, pulls you by the arm and starts yelling at you to hurry up because you have to be in the car in five minutes.

What do you feel? Probably **furious** that your fun has been stopped. **Resentful** because you had no warning. **Sad** because you were having such a wonderful time. All these negative feelings are erupting inside you, but you have no way to express them verbally.

So what do you do? There is only one way of letting the world know how totally enraged you feel. You throw yourself on the ground, kick your arms and legs in fury, aiming at any object that comes across your path (even if it's your mom's shins) and you refuse to budge.

And then what happens? Often, especially in those days of *children are seen and not heard,* the result is a smack on the butt, a loudly raised voice, or you are sternly yanked off to the 'naughty corner'.

So what happens to those very negative feelings? They build up to a crescendo. Parents' feelings also explode; everyone is exhausted and the whimpering two-year-old is no closer to learning that vital lesson – **the feeling is acceptable but the behaviour is not.**

We will get to the specifics of handling the behaviour later but for now, it is suffice to stress that:

> If the feeling is calmly and firmly contained, the toddler will feel understood and accepted and the behavioural outburst will quickly subside.

Restore equilibrium

Another unhelpful adult tendency is to try being rational and logical when the toddler, due to the intensity of her feelings, is actually totally lost to reason. Picture this scenario:

A toddler thrashing around the floor of the supermarket, yelling and sobbing for a sweet-treat. The embarrassed, desperate father (trying so hard to put his new-age-dad skills into practice) remains calm, gets down to the toddler's level and begins a mini-lecture about the bad things that happen to teeth, adding that the Tooth Fairy doesn't like teeth with holes in them. None of this is heard, let alone comprehended. In fact, the decibels of toddler anguish only get higher! The furious fellow needs dad to ditch the trolley for a while, pick him up firmly and walk to a quiet spot, saying gently but very simply, "I can see you feel angry when Dad says you can't have sweets." Although, in all likelihood, he won't suddenly cave in and smile happily at you, your calm, capable sense of containment will help him to regain his emotional equilibrium before too long.

Here I feel it is necessary to repeat the analogy of the 'Feeling Egg' from my *Children Need Boundaries* book:

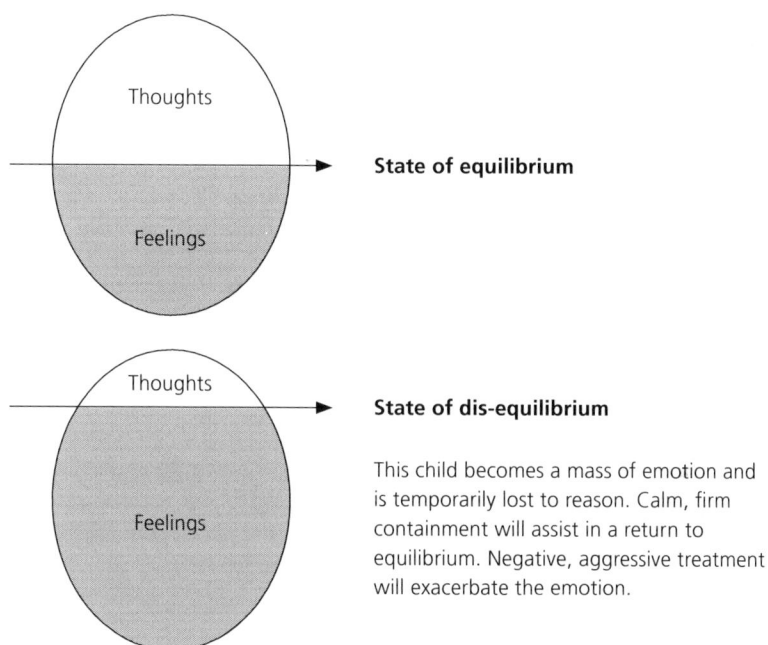

State of equilibrium

State of dis-equilibrium

This child becomes a mass of emotion and is temporarily lost to reason. Calm, firm containment will assist in a return to equilibrium. Negative, aggressive treatment will exacerbate the emotion.

This makes the point very clear. When the toddler is overcome by emotions, she has no 'space' for logical thought. Once the equilibrium is restored, there is once again a space for rationality but even then, this must be at a toddler level. I am reminded here of a quote from Haim Ginott's book, *Between Parent and Child* :

"When I ask you a small question, why do you give me such a long answer?" To his friends he confides, "I don't tell mother anything. If I start talking to her, I have no time left to play."

Granted, this was an older child, but the principle is still the same!

Act as a buffer

Remember the quote from Stephen Covey about stimulus and response? Your toddler will give you a thousand reasons to lose your cool every day. But remember that *you* are the adult and hopefully have the mature ability to react accordingly. Many years ago, during a Parent Effectiveness Group, an insightful mother with considerable artistic talent drew a couple of very graphic depictions. She drew a picture of a toddler in the throes of a tantrum – represented as a bomb-blast. The parent, unable to act as a container, was erupting with an even more volatile bomb-blast, which equalled double the incendiary impact.

The next picture was also of the toddler exploding, but in this one, the parent was depicted as a sandbag – fulfilling the important function of absorbing and detonating the blast!

So, when your toddler explodes, visualise yourself as an effective, bomb-detonating sandbag. You may not like this view of yourself, but it really does work!

All you are doing is absorbing the feelings, and helping him develop the important life-skill of being able to verbalise them once he becomes emotionally capable of doing so. I have to add a little jibe here … I know many adults who would do well to learn this ability too and I believe they would have, had they had the benefit of this type of effective parenting.

WHAT ABOUT THE GOOD FEELINGS?

My examples have all, it seems, been on the side of angry and aggressive feelings – possibly because toddlers are in a very negative life-stage. But obviously, learning a rich and varied vocabulary for feelings involves the full range of human emotions. It is a matter of ensuring you are connecting; that you take the time and effort to de-code their toddler behaviour. This means also ensuring that you remember that most of communication is non-verbal anyway.

So, when your toddler looks despondent as she searches for her precious baby doll, you can practice your decoding skills. "I see a very sad little Hannah, let me help look for baby Jess." Or, when two-year-old Kyle bursts into heartbroken sobs because the wheel came off his special car, try saying, "I can see you are very upset … let's see if we can put it back on."

Then there are all the joyful, happy toddler feelings. You see Abigail's incredulous look of joy as she opens her birthday presents and say, "I can see that you are overjoyed and happy. Birthdays are such fun!" Or, as dad comes though the arrivals hall at the airport, after an overseas business trip, "Look, Brent, here comes Daddy. Isn't it exciting?"

So how does that make you feel?

Your use of as many *feeling* words as possible during this window of opportunity (when they are trying to make sense of so much in their toddler world), will help them get in touch with feelings and learn to express them as they mature emotionally. The rewarding outcome is that, when they can express themselves more accurately, they will correct you if your decoding skills are slightly off the mark. I vividly remember an occasion when I called my four-year-old son (now 23) for his bath. He came in looking like thunder and stomped up the stairs. I remarked, "Goodness, what an angry guy you are." To which Greg replied, "I'm not angry. I'm very, very sad." Do you see how amazingly it can work?

There is absolutely no doubt that children who have a rich vocabulary for 'feeling' words have a head start in life. In the case of the more volatile, challenging children especially, the ability to express strong feelings will almost certainly minimize the need for ventilation via unacceptable behaviour.

Common mistakes made by well-intentioned adults

One of the biggest mistakes adults make, when attempting to help their children to get in touch with their feelings, is the habit of asking too many direct questions. "Why are you crying? What's the matter? Stop yelling and just tell me what you want." Or, "I can't hear you when you scream at me. What on earth is the problem?"

The problem with this type of questioning is that:

• It is a closed communication technique, so does not encourage an open response.
• It is confrontational: instead of encouraging communication, it blocks it.
• It does not help the toddler to understand what he is feeling.
• He certainly has no idea why he is feeling that way!

Remember the 'feeling egg'. By asking direct questions the adult is using a rational approach during a time when the toddler, overcome by strong feelings, is totally unable to understand 'why' – let alone answer the question!

So remember to avoid direct questions when your toddler is in a state of emotional disequilibrium. Rather use calm, reflective, open-ended techniques, which will de-escalate the tension and help your toddler to feel understood, and learn to label her feelings eventually. This is the core of emotional intelligence: being able to identify feelings accurately, and then learning how to express them appropriately.

"Emotional Intelligence is the master aptitude, a capacity that profoundly affects all other abilities, either facilitating them or interfering with them."

Daniel Goleman: *Emotional Intelligence*

SUMMARY OF CHAPTER 6

- The ability to get in touch with feelings – and to express them appropriately – is the cornerstone of emotional intelligence.
- The only way toddlers know how to express their strong feelings is behaviourally. They do not yet possess adequate verbal skills.
- Parents have no problem labelling objects for babies, yet find it difficult to label their feelings.
- An emotionally connected parent, who has empathy for their baby/toddler, will develop the ability to decode the behaviour … to get in touch with the underlying feeling.
- When a toddler becomes embroiled in strong feelings, it is essential for the parent to remain calm in order to help restore the toddler's equilibrium. The effective parent of a toddler will act as a buffer – and will learn to react in ways that will be helpful to the toddler.
- The tendency in adults to ask direct questions when a toddler is in a state of 'an emotional blown fuse', will not help her feel contained or understood, nor will it help her to learn the words for her feelings.
- The key to effective handling of toddlers is to understand this important rule: **Feelings are always acceptable – but behaviour sometimes is not.**
- *"Having an empathic parent is possibly the greatest gift a child can be given,"* taken from my book, *Children Need Boundaries.*

7

Holding up a mirror

HOW SELF-ESTEEM IS DEVELOPED

> "You and I – we meet as strangers, each carrying a mystery within us. I cannot say who you are. I may never know you completely. But I trust that you are a person in your own right, possessed of a beauty and value that are the Earth's richest treasures. So I make this promise to you: I will impose no identities upon you, but will invite you to become yourself without shame or fear. I will hold open a space for you in the world and allow your right to fill it with an authentic vocation and purpose. For as long as your search takes, you have my loyalty."
>
> Author unknown: Extract from *Peace Education Manual*

There is no doubt that a toddler/child who feels good is more likely to behave well. Therefore, I would like to emphasize the importance of self-esteem formation as a precursor for effective discipline. It used to be believed, by well-meaning and knowledgeable adults, that a child's personality was formed in the first five years. While the first five years are crucial for personality and self-concept development, we now know that this is, in fact, a life-long process. However, there is no doubt that it becomes more and more challenging to change the negative influences of those early years. Therefore, as parents of babies and toddlers, you are in a powerful position to influence your little one's self-esteem positively, and thereby give her a most precious gift … one which will stand her in good stead her whole life.

> "Helping children build high self esteem is the key to successful parenthood."
>
> Dorothy Corkille Briggs: *Your Child's Self-Esteem*

CAREGIVERS AS MIRRORS

Newborn babies have no perception of their individuality or separateness. They are totally dependent for their every need, and the way in which they develop a sense of their worth as a unique and separate being, is largely as a result of the way in which they see themselves mirrored via the verbal and non-verbal reactions of their important caregivers.

Let us look for a few minutes at baby Katy:

Katy's mother responds warmly to her needs. She holds her close during feeds, coos at her and looks into her eyes. She is relaxed and her tone of voice is soft and gentle. During bath-time, this mother laughs when Katy splashes the water, and therefore Katy sees and feels her mother's warm connectedness. She begins to get a sense of being loved and valued.

However, if Katy has a mother who is preoccupied at feeding time, fails to make eye contact, puts her down quickly and gets through bath-time without any sense of genuine enjoyment or positive connection, Katy would develop a very different set of impressions about herself than she would with the first kind of mother.

They see themselves reflected

Right from birth, babies see themselves reflected in these figurative mirrors – and thus the foundations for their future self-concepts are laid. I must hasten to stress that it cannot only be positive reflections they see, but it is the overall picture that counts.

Many mothers who have suffered from post-natal depression (PND) share that they feel guilty because they were unable to reflect predominantly positive feelings during that very difficult time. However, these babies will usually have received very positive reflections from fathers, grandparents and/or other caring people, so will have received very affirming messages. And these moms will definitely be able to make up for any deficits once their depression is diagnosed and treated.

As the baby grows towards toddlerhood, so do the factors that influence the growth of healthy self-esteem, and these parental mirrors reflect back to him in ever-increasingly powerful ways. We have already discussed some of the vital factors in previous chapters:

- The child's **genetically-determined temperament**.
- **Avoidance of the insidious downward cycle of negative labelling**. If a toddler sees herself reflected as 'bad', 'naughty', 'aggressive', 'bully', 'nasty' etc. In short, a litany of negative adjectives, this is how he will come to view himself. Conversely, if he sees the reflection of a 'determined', 'assertive', 'friendly', 'fun' and 'happy' boy, this is how he will come to see himself.
- **Acceptance of the characteristics of a toddler**. He is not 'naughty' when he has a tantrum or refuses to eat his fish fingers. He is doing what toddlers do!
- **Feelings always come before behaviour** – and the feelings are acceptable, although maybe the behaviour is not. Acceptance of feelings is a crucial element of self-esteem formation.

ADDITIONAL FACTORS VITAL TO THE DEVELOPMENT OF POSITIVE SELF-CONCEPT IN TODDLERS

Unrealistic expectations

It often strikes me how often well-intentioned adults fall into this trap:

SCENARIO 1

Granny's 60th birthday lunch at a 5-star restaurant: The whole family is gathered to-gether, having a couple of drinks and a happy conversation. Two-and-a-half-year-old Brent is the centre of adult attention as he plays, runs and shows off his new Super-man toy. Then the family sits down for the celebratory meal. Brent is tired and hungry by now and is seated on his toddler booster seat. He immediately grabs a roll, breaks it into pieces, then becomes restless and wants to change seats. Mom and dad get irritated – they so badly want the family to see what a 'star' child they are raising. Dad becomes stern and Brent's voice rises. Mom entreats him (in urgent whispers) to be "a good boy, then you can have sweeties later." Brent could not care less and begins to yell loudly, adamantly refusing to sit at the table … and the tension rises!

Unrealistic expectation: That a two-and-a-half-year-old can sit quietly at an adult birthday lunch.
Solution: Either leave Brent at home with a babysitter or ensure that someone reliable is available to care for him during the lunch.

SCENARIO 2

Jessica has just had her second birthday and is very possessive of some of her new toys. It's her mom's turn to host the other four children in their informal weekly playgroup. When they arrive, Jessica becomes extremely upset when they immediately begin playing with these new toys. Her embarrassed mom begs her to 'be nice', saying, "Jessica, we need to share our toys." Jessica becomes enraged and throws herself on the floor, weeping inconsolably.

Unrealistic expectation: That two-year-olds can share. It is developmentally normal not to!
Solution: Pack away the precious new toys and only put out the 'playgroup' toys.

SCENARIO 3

You have been visiting your in-laws for tea. Nearly-three-year-old Jason has played happily and it has been a pleasant and relaxed visit. When it's time to leave, you say to him, "Jason, say thank you to Nanna and Gramps." Jason looks at the ground and stubbornly refuses! Nanna and Gramps look hurt and upset. "Didn't you have a good time?" they ask. Jason continues to stare at the ground, beginning to look more and more upset.

Unrealistic expectation: That nearly-three-year-olds will have developed social 'niceties'. These skills take a while – by the age of seven or eight they should have got there.
Solution: When you see the resistance, avoid the power struggle and verbalise for him: "I'm sure Jason has had a lovely time, he's just a bit tired and shy now. Thank you so much Nanna and Gramps."

Input
All the above situations, badly handled, can lead to a lowering of self-esteem. Handled age-appropriately, the self-concept remains intact.

> *"If you live with youngsters so that you can crush self-esteem, you thwart positive growth; in fact you foster warped, defensive development."*
>
> Dorothy Corkille Briggs: *Your Child's Self-Esteem*

Do not over-control

Remember that the core issue in the development of autonomy, which is the main challenge for the toddler's healthy personality development, is that they need to feel that they have a measure of control in their lives.

Forcing them to eat, insisting that they sit on the potty and go to sleep when you put them to bed. Insisting that they wear what we say they should and do exactly as we tell them … all of these over-controlling absolute orders will only escalate power struggles and leave them feeling totally disempowered.

These examples, and how to handle them, will be dealt with in more detail later. At this stage though, it suffices to impress on you that forcing your toddler to conform to your way, and not giving her reasonable choices within clear and realistic boundaries, will slowly, but surely, erode at her sense of being worthwhile.

> *"Every child seeks a self-picture as capable and strong. And behaviour matches the self-image."*
>
> Dorothy Corkille Briggs: *Your Child's Self-Esteem*

Beware the trap of over-enthusiastic 'pushing'

It is so tempting, as a new and enthusiastic parent, to grab at any early signs of 'childhood genius'! Woe betide the two-year-old who shows a precocious ability in any direction …

SITUATION 1

Little Isabella, still rather wobbly and uncoordinated, seems to show an early penchant for ballet. She points her toes beautifully and jumps lightly on her feet. So she is rushed off to buy a tiny pair of ballet shoes and a leotard and is enrolled in toddler ballet class. Granny comes along to watch her second lesson. Isabella is overcome – it is all too much for her – and she totally refuses to be separated from Mom and Granny.

Possible outcome: It is four years before she will even look at a pair of ballet shoes again!

SITUATION 2

Joshua, at just over two-years-old, seems very adept at his baby-type puzzles. Mom and Dad are excited and rush off to buy more advanced puzzles. They sit him down and eagerly encourage this bright little guy to try the more difficult ones. He battles but his parents encourage/push him to persevere. Joshua feels discouraged and bored, quickly losing interest. His parents become more forceful and utter phrases like, "We are only trying to stimulate and encourage him," or, "He seemed so good at it."

Possible outcome: Joshua avoids puzzles, after all, when he enjoyed the ones he found fun and interesting, he was given ones he could not manage. An unintentional blow to this toddler's fragile self-image.

Avoid evaluative praise

Being positive, and looking for qualities and behaviour to praise, is a vital part of showing your toddler reflections of herself which are wonderful, special and unique. However, it is all too easy to develop the habit of praising evaluatively: "You clever girl," or, "What a beautiful picture." These enthusiastic responses are normal and unavoidable, as proud and loving parents bask in their toddler's early achievements and mastery of new skills.

As toddlers grow and develop, it is important to practise descriptive praise. This has two components:
- The adult describes, with appreciation, what he sees and feels.
- The child, after hearing the descriptive praise, can praise himself.

Let's look at our ballet dancer and puzzle whizz-kids:

ADULT DESCRIPTION	CHILD'S SELF-PRAISE
It is so exciting to see such lovely pointed toes and beautiful jumps. ⟶	I am a good dancer – this is something I do well.
Goodness Joshua, you certainly can do puzzles quickly. That is so clever.	It feels good to build puzzles so well. I want to do more.

The lesson: Without diminishing spontaneity, when you take the trouble to **describe** rather than merely **evaluate**, you develop the very important skill of showing your child that it is **what** he does that is praiseworthy. When you tell a little person often enough that he is capable of these positive things, these become solid building blocks in his self-image. He then sees positive reflections in that parental mirror. Once you have described something positive you cannot nullify it. "It was so nice to see how gentle you were with the baby," becomes an indelible impression in the toddler's memory bank – even if he has to be reprimanded for behaving badly five minutes later!

Remember … we all need to hear something positive about ourselves every day, and toddlers need hefty doses of this, especially the more challenging ones. However, it is the **way** that the adults praise the child that is important.

> "Even positive evaluations (praise) works against safety, for all judgments put the child in the position of living with a labeller. It doesn't take a child – or any of us long to know that if a person can evaluate positively, he can also evaluate negatively."
>
> Dorothy Corkille Briggs: *Your Child's Self-Esteem*

Avoid the stressed, busy, frenetic whirlpool

One of the most effective, and lasting, ways to build and cement a good sense of self-belief is when an important person takes the time, and makes the effort, to reinforce the feeling that, "I am important and special to you."

It is so easy for busy and stressed parents to get out of sync with their toddlers because we have such different priorities and perceptions.

Parents are usually rushing to get to the next deadline or commitment but toddlers have no sense of time urgency yet. A ladybird on the pavement is far more important than the supermarket closing in ten minutes.

Parents get involved and forget that toddlers need to be warned about time. Telling them that their sand play with a friend has to end abruptly, because you suddenly realize you're late to fetch an older sibling from school, does not go down well.

Some tips for parents of toddlers

- Think ahead – and factor in a toddler's different timeframe.
- View their world as important too. That ladybird on the pavement is very important. Crouch down, look at it, describe its colours and help it to a safer spot. It will only take a minute or two, and you'll still make it to the supermarket before closing. And if you don't, maybe you will remember to allow more time in future!
- Even though you'd rather continue watching your TV show, go and sit on the floor, make eye-contact and join in your toddler's game.
- In spite of feeling exhausted and stressed, take off your shoes, run on the lawn, play with the sprinkler on a hot day, put on a CD and dance, laugh and play – in short, be

a toddler. Not only will your stress levels come down, but you will be saying to this precious little person, "You are special to me and I love doing things with you."

> "Focused attention – direct involvement – all hereness; it is a quality that gets love across. It nourishes self-respect at the roots because it says 'I care'." "We don't ordinarily feel unloved when we lack exclusive attention. It is when others never have time to be truly with us that we feel unimportant."
>
> Dorothy Corkille Briggs: *Your Child's Self-Esteem*

- Avoid labelling, judgemental, you-language. This diminishes, erodes and crushes the very soul of self-esteem, and is the subject of the next Chapter.

To end this discussion on the ways in which important adults hold up mirrors to children, I found this lovely story entitled *The Little Boy*. It says so much, and although the boy is no longer a toddler, the principles of the story are relevant.

THE LITTLE BOY

Once a little boy went to school. He was a quiet little boy. And it was quite a big school. But when the little boy found he could go to his room by walking right in from the door outside, he was happy. And school did not seem quite so big any more.

One morning when the boy had been in school for a while, the teacher said, "Today we are going to make a picture." "Good," thought the little boy. He liked to make pictures. He could make all kinds; lions and tigers; chickens and cows; trains and boats. And he took out his box of crayons and began to draw.

But the teacher said: "Wait! It is not time to begin!" And she waited until everyone looked ready. "Now," said the teacher, "we are going to make flowers." "Good!" thought the little boy. He liked to make flowers. And he began to make beautiful ones with his pink and orange and blue crayons.

But the teacher said, "Wait and I will show you how." And she drew a flower on the blackboard. It was red, with a green stem. "There," said the teacher. "Now you may begin."

The little boy looked at the teacher's flower. Then he looked at his own flower. He liked his flower better than the teacher's. But he did not say this. He just turned his paper over and made a flower like the teacher's. It was red, with a green stem.

On another day when the little boy had opened the door from the outside all by himself, the teacher said: "Today we are going to make something with clay. "Good!" thought the little boy. He liked clay. He could make all sorts of things with clay; snakes and snowmen; elephants and mice; cars and trucks. And he began to pull and pinch his ball of clay.

But the teacher said: "Wait! It is not time to begin!" And she waited until everyone looked ready. "Now," said the teacher, "we are going to make a dish." "Good!" thought the little boy. He liked to make dishes. And he began to make some that were all shapes and sizes.

But the teacher said, "Wait and I will show you how." And she showed everyone how to make one deep dish. "There," said the teacher, "now you may begin."

The little boy looked at the teacher's dish. Then he looked at his own. He liked his dish better than the teacher's. But he did not say this. He just rolled his clay into a big ball again. And made a dish like the teacher's. It was a deep dish.

And pretty soon the little boy learnt to wait and to watch. And to make things just like the teacher. And pretty soon he didn't make things of his own any more.

Then it happened that the little boy and his family moved to another house in another city. And the little boy had to go to another school.

This school was even bigger than the other one. And there was no door from the outside into his room. He had to go up some big steps and walk down a long hall to get to his room.

And the very first day he was there, the teacher said: "Today we are going to make a picture." "Good!" thought the little boy, and he waited for the teacher to tell him what to do. But the teacher didn't say anything. She just walked around the room.

When she came to the little boy, she said: "Don't you want to make a picture?" "Yes," said the little boy. "What are we going to make?" "I don't know until you make it," said the teacher. "How shall I make it?" asked the little boy. "Why, any way you like," said the teacher. "And any colour?" asked the little boy. "Any colour," said the teacher. "If everyone made the same picture and used the same colours, how would I know who made what, and which was which?" "I don't know," said the little boy. And he began to make pink and orange and blue flowers.

He liked his new school. Even if it didn't have a door right in from the outside.

Helen Buckley: *Centre for Conflict Resolution*

The moral of this lovely story? Allow children to develop their unique talents and creativity. Do not over-control and project your own expectations on them. Within the very necessary containment of limits and boundaries, allow the freedom of age-appropriate choice. The teacher at the first school was crushing the boy's spirit and in so doing was eroding at the very core of his self-belief.

....

SUMMARY OF CHAPTER 7

- Adults hold up mirrors in which the children see themselves reflected. If they see reflections which depict them as predominantly 'bad', 'naughty', 'rude' etc, this is the way they will see themselves, and they will, in all likelihood, develop a negative view of themselves.
- Even newborn babies begin to pick up positive or negative 'vibes', which send very powerful messages about how they are loved and accepted.
- Vital factors in self-esteem formation:
  - Understanding of the child's temperament.
  - Avoidance of negative labelling – look for positives.
  - Knowledge of normal toddler behaviour.
  - Feelings are always acceptable, although some behaviour may not be.
  - Avoid tendencies to over-control by giving absolute orders.
  - Allow the toddler to develop at his own pace: never push him to achieve beyond his capabilities.
  - Use descriptive praise – avoid lavish, evaluative praise.
  - Take time to get down to your toddler's level … relax and enjoy him. This says, "You are important to me."

8

Parents have feelings too

TODDLER-FRIENDLY ANGER MANAGEMENT

Aristotle, the well-known philosopher, is reputed to have said:

"Anyone can become angry – that is easy. But to be angry with the right person, to the right degree, at the right time, for the right purpose, and in the right way – this is not easy."

The very nature of toddlers makes them lovable, adorable and amazing: they are learning so much and each day seems to bring new and exciting developments. They are beginning to verbalise their needs and to share in the excitement of the world around them. They can run and climb, push and jump. They can feed themselves and are proud of their ability to go to the toilet alone. But they have also learnt the power of the word 'no'; that they can express feelings via aggression; that they can get their way by screaming and yelling, and that parents are inconsistent and can be easily manipulated!

So, what do parents of these beautiful, exhausting, exasperating mini-dynamos do when they reach the end of their tether? When they have tried their utmost to follow the steps outlined in the previous seven chapters, but begin to ask, "What about me? Am I allowed to have bad days or mood-swings? In short, am I allowed to be human?"

The answer is most definitely yes! But handle it with care and skill. So, how do you express frustration, irritation and anger without denting this demanding toddler's self-esteem? By reading this chapter very carefully and committing to, and internalising, the skill of assertive I-language!

WHY TODDLERS BECOME PARENT DEAF

In order to learn more effective ways to express negative emotions, it is useful to begin by looking at what we do wrong:
- **Parents of toddlers say, "No," far too easily**. We know this is the case because *no* is one of the first words they learn – and they learnt it from us! They are eager and

energetic. The world is an exciting place full of new objects and experiences. Pot plants to pull out, knobs to push, toys to throw, other children to shove, smack and bite: all adding up to a constant need for adults to chant a constant litany of *No*.

- **Parents become frustrated** when their attempts at limiting unacceptable behaviour become ineffective in the face of the toddler's inner drive to go on touching, pressing, shoving and pulling! Adults then resort to shouting and yelling. After saying, "No," ten times, the next level is to shout at the toddler. This only leads to:
  - a power struggle,
  - anxiety and fear,
  - crushing of the toddler's spirit, and
  - an increase in adult stress-levels.
- **Labelling and name-calling**. When saying, "No," or shouting and yelling seem to have no effect, the second-last resort is to label the child judgementally. "You naughty boy." "You nasty, mean little bully." "How could you ruin my best plant – you are driving me crazy!"

Break the habit

This is where the habit of using you-language begins. We are furious, exhausted – at the end of our tether, so we very easily begin to label the child's personality, rather than expressing how the **behaviour** makes us feel.

And this is where it all goes so horribly wrong … so, just for a few minutes, put yourself in the shoes of the average two-year-old.

Jamie is two-and-a-half years old. She already shows signs of having a very determined, strong-willed temperament. At this age she is in the stage of wanting to feel that she is in control; that she has the power to make choices and she has also learnt that, if she tries hard enough, she is able to get her own way. Jamie finds the world new and exciting. She loves touching things in the shops; running after birds in the park; making a mess with water and sand and getting herself covered in paint while she experiments with all of her finger paints.

However, the adults in her life have problems with all of this. They begin to say, "No," to all the exciting things she wants to try. When she carries on making mud pies in the garden or spilling paint on her clothes, they say, "No," even more vehemently. The urge to go on having fun is just too big to stop immediately, so then they shout at her to stop. She just wants to make one more pattern with the paint, but they then yell at her and call her *naughty* and *defiant*. However, she also learns that they often go on and on with their threats and reprimands (which are not effective in helping her to learn more effective behaviour), so she begins to learn to filter some of this out. The shouting, Nos and you-language become like the wallpaper on your computer screen; just there in the background! But the really damaging effect of this negative communication is to exacerbate power struggles and decrease the possibility of effective discipline in the future.

THE POWER OF I-LANGUAGE

Many parents feel that the use of I-language should only really apply to the older child, that babies and toddlers would be impervious to the real value of this skill. However, the sooner parents become adept at the use of 'I' rather than 'you' communication, the better. There is no doubt that the 'you' comes far easier, probably because this is the way adults have automatically spoken to children for centuries. It is vitally important to practice the 'I-skill' – not only on your toddler, but also on your partner and in all interpersonal communication.

The positive spin-offs from using the 'I-feel' rather than 'you are' language:

- It is respectful.
- It role models an emotionally intelligent way to express negative emotions.
- It deals with the situation or the behaviour and not the personality.
- It separates the deed from the doer.
- It is clear and specific.
- It does not erode self-esteem.

Practical application

Essentially the format for I-language is as follows:

Instead of ventilating angrily by blaming, judging and name-calling, as in, "You drive me mad. You never tidy up your toys," rather express the **feeling** that the **behaviour** evokes in you. "I feel very irritated when I see toys all over the floor."

The essence of I-language is that *there is* a strong negative feeling and it is important not to bottle up this feeling, but the feeling needs to be expressed in a non-damaging way. Essentially it is okay to be angry, but not to take this out in behaviourally unacceptable ways.

TODDLER-TYPE I-LANGUAGE		
SITUATION	**YOU-LANGUAGE**	**I-LANGUAGE**
Two-year-old spills juice on the carpet.	You clumsy boy! Look what you've done!	I feel frustrated when I see juice on the carpet.
Your toddler pinches her friend hard while playing.	Lucy, you are such a little bully.	Lucy, I feel very upset when Milly is so sad.
Three-year-old pulls his granny's first precious tulip out of the pot.	Now look what you've done! You naughty boy.	I feel very angry when Gran's special plant is pulled out.

THE PROBLEMS

Toddlers are egocentric

There is one stumbling block – toddlers are still almost totally egocentric. This means that they really do not have the ability to feel empathy for the feelings of others, in fact, they really couldn't care less! Their egocentricity means that they are wrapped up in themselves, so when a parent, endeavouring to practice their new-found I-message skills says, "I get very frustrated when I see toys everywhere," it is like water off a duck's back. Your toddler will remain impervious to your good intentions!

The main benefit at this stage is that you are training yourselves to communicate your strong feelings in this very mature and emotionally intelligent manner. It is far easier to practise while your child is still a toddler. It is never too late to learn new skills, but it does become more challenging as children grow older. I well remember my somewhat erratic first attempts at switching from my automatic you-language to my newly learnt vocabulary of I-language, only to be met with the startled remark from a surprised child: "Why are you talking in such a funny way, Mom?" When they are toddlers they have not yet become accustomed to negative and ineffective parental responses!

It can induce guilt

Many a parent has raised this concern. "But if I keep telling my toddler how his behaviour makes me feel, won't I make the poor little guy feel too guilty?"

Well, it all depends on how you do it. If you overdo it, you very well could cause your toddler to develop an over-intense conscience. For instance, if a furious two-year-old stamps her feet angrily and yells, "No, go away!" And the furious parent replies, "Oh no, I feel so sad and upset when I am shouted at. I love you so much and would do anything for you. Please don't spoil my day." The bewildered toddler probably won't understand most of it, but the basic theme of guilt-overdose will filter through.

However, effectively communicated, age-appropriate I-language gently eases children towards an understanding of how their behaviour impacts on others; a crucial ingredient of healthy personality development, which includes age-appropriate conscience development, whilst ensuring that self-esteem remains positively intact.

"Negative judgements make you a negative mirror for children. More important, they play havoc with self-respect and safety. They belittle, shame and chastise, they make children feel unloved. Sharing appropriate inner reactions about behaviour on the other hand, does not whittle down self-respect, undermine safety, nor erode love."

"Blame – negative judgement – is at the core of emotional disorder and low self-esteem."

"Imagine being a child and having the remarks in the two columns below sent your way. What are your reactions? Which group of statements takes you down a notch?

A	B
"You're impossible."	"I can't stand all this bickering."
"You're lazy."	"I don't want to keep picking up your toys."
"You bad boy."	"It hurts little Mike when he's pinched. I don't like to see him hurt."

It cannot be emphasized too strongly, that judgments are troublemakers. The secret for safety is to react but to suspend judgment."

Dorothy Corkille Briggs: *Your Child's Self-Esteem*

ABBREVIATED TODDLER-TYPE MESSAGES

Although it is beneficial to get into the I-language habit, toddler behaviour is often immediate and irrational and demands immediate, clear responses. Instead of the usual process of 'no', raised voices and you-labels, try the following responses, stated firmly and very clearly:

"That wasn't a nice way to behave."

"We don't hurt people."

"Toys are not for throwing."

"Plants need to stay in the garden."

"It's not kind to pull the cat's tail."

In these examples, although not expressing any actual feelings (a key aspect of a theoretically correct I-message) the parent is staying firmly focused on the situation or behaviour, with no overlong embellishments or 'side shows'.

In all of the above examples, the adult is practising that essential Stephen Covey skill: *"Between stimulus and response …"* The adult is then reacting firmly, but calmly. No need for endless 'nos', impatient shouting and yelling, and unnecessary, debilitating put-downs, name-calling, sarcasm and humiliation. All that is necessary is the mature and effective ability to stick with the main issue, which is the unacceptable behaviour.

That last resort!

I have outlined the usual process of rapid parental meltdown:

• saying *no* constantly

• shouting and yelling

• name-calling and harsh punishment

Another one that has yet to be mentioned (but is the usual end-result for frazzled parents) is the inevitable smack. This brings us to the most crucial part of the process: **to smack or not to smack,** and most importantly, the reasons why this should not even be an option. So, read on …

SUMMARY OF CHAPTER 8

- Parents can conscientiously follow all the skills and suggestions outlined thus far, but will inevitably reach the point where firmer action is required, and age-appropriate boundaries need to be set. Parents have needs and feelings too, and the right to assert them.
- In order to understand why toddlers (and older children) become 'parent-deaf', the following parental mistakes need to be outlined:

   Parents say too many 'nos' to their curious, energetic and enthusiastic toddlers. They then begin shouting and yelling when the 'nos' fall on 'deaf' toddler ears. The shouting and yelling is usually accompanied by name-calling and judgemental 'you-language'.

- Developing the skills of using **I-language** when experiencing negative emotions is more respectful; it is a powerful, positive role-modelling skill; it separates the deed from the doer; it is clear and specific and it does not erode self-esteem.
- Parents need to be aware of possible pitfalls though. Toddlers are egocentric and don't really care how others feel. This may lead parents to feel it is ineffective. Over-use can lead to unnecessary feelings of guilt.
- Try using more specific language, for example, "We don't hurt people," "Toys are not meant to be thrown," or, "It is not kind to pull the cat's tail."
- Use of clear and specific expressions of limits regarding unacceptable behaviour will set the foundations for more effective discipline in the future.

Let us now proceed to that crucial question which parents of toddlers repeatedly ask parenting counsellors, psychologists, other parents, teachers, etc …"**To smack or not to smack?**"

9

To smack or not to smack

THIS IS THE VITAL TODDLER QUESTION

"Just a little tap on the hand or on his nappy, surely this can't do any harm?"

"How else can you get through to a challenging, stubborn toddler?"

"I try so hard to be calm and patient. But he just goes on doing exactly as he wants. I then become more volatile but he *still* does what he wants. So then I have to get tougher, and I give him a smack on his bum."

"I really don't believe in smacking but what about all those really dangerous items and situations? Things like a hot stove, an open fire, plugs or running into the road. There comes a time when only a smack will help."

And so it goes on … justification, explanations and excuses!

The problem is that many parents truly believe that this is effective discipline. It is at this toddler stage (when the child's inner drive is directed towards exploration and testing, and the parents' is towards obedience and order) that the early foundations for future discipline problems are laid. Many parents, who readily concede that smacks and hidings are not effective in older children, can see no harm in smacking a toddler. Essentially, it does not appear to be such a big deal, especially if the toddler-type smack is meant as a firm deterrent and not as harsh and abusive punishment. Many a well-intentioned parent of a toddler has assured me, "Of course I won't go on smacking once I can reason with him properly."

THE PROBLEMS WITH SMACKING

Before getting into the smacking habit – often without conscious intention – it is important to keep an open mind regarding the possibility that you can raise a well-disciplined child who has never been spanked. It is important to reflect on some of the obvious problems with smacking.

- **Remember that your toddler is learning about behaviour** and will model her behaviour on what she observes from the adult role-models in her life. If she observes that these important adults shout, yell and smack when they want her to behave in certain ways, this is exactly how she will behave when she wants people (usually other toddlers) to do what she wants them to do. So when she shouts and smacks the children at Toddlers Workshop, she is surely only imitating what adults have taught her to do when she runs out of other options!

> "Children learn best through parental modelling. Punishment gives the message that hitting is an appropriate way to express one's feelings and to solve problems. If the child rarely sees the adult handle anger and solve problems in a creative and positive way, he can never learn how to do that himself. This inadequate parenting continues into the next generation."
>
> Jan Hunt: *Ten Reasons Not To Hit Your Kid*, reprinted by permission of *End Physical Punishment of Children (EPPOCH)*

- Due to their age and stage of development, **toddlers have levels of innate aggression**, which they have not yet learnt to channel in socially acceptable ways. The chances are that giving smacks for behaviour that is often the direct result of unchannelled anger, will only exacerbate the anger and escalate the cycles of aggression.

> "**Punishment greatly interferes with the bond between parent and child**, as no human being feels loving towards someone who deliberately hurts him or her. The true co-operative behaviour the parent desires can only be accomplished through a strong bond based on loving feelings, and through examples of kindness and co-operative skills. Punishment, even when it appears to work, can produce only superficially 'good' behaviour based on fear."
>
> Jan Hunt: *Ten Reasons Not To Hit Your Kid*
> [*End Physical Punishment of Children (EPPOCH)*]

- Another very unfortunate problem with smacking is that **it has a drug-effect**. In other words, parents often have to increase the dose in order to get the same effect. A 'little smack' on a toddler's hand can become a harder smack on his bottom, then a hiding and from there, sadly, a very hard smack with a ruler, slipper or wooden spoon. Often it will be the same parent who, two or three years earlier, had firmly stated that the 'gentle smack' given to a defiant toddler would not become a habit once she was older.
- **Smacking can escalate power-struggles and defiance**. In the case of the more challenging toddler (and then older child), smacks just do not work. Over the years countless parents have assured me, "I only had to give him a good smack once and he never drew on the walls again." Or, "When she bit another toddler at playgroup, all I had to do was to bite her back and she never did it again."

Apart from the vital principles that 'two wrongs don't make a right' and 'never treat aggression with aggression', my experience is that these examples are of temperamentally amenable children. Those with more challenging temperaments will only become more aggressive and defiant. This is a sad state of affairs for the possibility of developing effective discipline skills.

- **Smacking causes feelings of resentment and humiliation**. Hitting another person cannot be condoned, no matter how small, powerless and immature that person happens to be. If another adult irritates, defies or challenges us and we choose to hit them, we could very well face legal action. So why even start smacking a toddler in the name of discipline? Toddlers do not yet have the verbal skills to express their feelings. When they are smacked for bad behaviour, they have no way to ventilate any possible feelings of anger and resentment. The only possible way would surely be to express their negative feelings behaviourally, which will then surely lead to an ongoing need to smack them for this behaviour. Not a very mature way for an adult to teach a toddler to behave appropriately! It is also disrespectful to strike another person for any reason. Remember, we are our toddler's role-models, we expect them to learn to respect us … yet we wonder why children seem to act so disrespectfully. We must hold up figurative mirrors to ourselves and ask: "Am I a good role-model? Am I worthy of my toddler's respect?" Toddlers often behave badly simply because they are responding to the (usually unintentional) neglect of some or other basic need. Perhaps they are overtired, hungry, thirsty, in need of exercise, space and fresh air, over-stimulated or frustrated by being over-controlled.

> "But his greatest need is for his parent's undivided attention. In these busy times, few children receive sufficient time and attention from their parents, who are often too tired, distracted to treat their children with patience and understanding. Punishing a child for responding in a natural way to having had important needs neglected, is really unfair."
>
> Jan Hunt: *Ten Reasons Not To Hit Your Kid*
> [End Physical Punishment of Children (EPPOCH)]

Negatives always have positives too! Therefore, smacking a toddler must surely have some positive effects? The only one I have ever been able to identify is that it temporarily alleviates parental stress, but this is often very quickly followed by guilt and regret.

So why do we go on doing it if it is so obviously harmful and ineffective in the long term?

Because it was done to us, and we blindly repeat these patterns without actually considering whether more effective parenting skills would bring better results.

- Many parents (especially fathers) who experienced their fair share of 'good, old-fashioned corporal punishment' are adamant that 'it did me no harm – I seem to be okay'. The truth is that in counselling practices such as mine, I see the true results of ineffective parenting. Too many adults are cut off from their own feelings, unable to show empathy, have low self-esteem and rely on unhelpful crutches such as medication, alcohol and illegal drugs in order to cope with life. I often am tempted to ask, "Did it really do you no harm?"
- Then there are those who feel adamant that because corporal punishment has been abolished in schools, we are seeing chaos in the world. And parents will add, "If I smack my defiant, aggressive toddler, hopefully he will learn to behave and won't need hidings when he's older. If not, he'll get hidings when he grows older too." I can assure even the most cynical parent that the chaos is not caused by taking away harsh, external punishment, but because adults have no idea about the real meaning of true discipline, and therefore have not developed more effective, intelligent and mature ways of teaching children to learn from the consequences of the choices they make.
- Some believe it to be a basic religious belief. I have been told repeatedly. "Spare the rod and spoil the child." In other words, if the Bible tells me it is okay, then it must be. My best answer to this is in the words of Jan Hunt:

> "The oft-quoted 'Spare the rod and spoil the child' is in fact a misinterpretation of biblical teaching. Although the rod is mentioned many times in the Bible, it is only in the Book of Proverbs (the words of King Solomon) that it is used in connection with child rearing. Solomon's methods worked very badly for his own son, Prince Rehoboham. In the Bible, there is no support for hitting children outside Solomon's Proverbs. Jesus saw children as being close to God and urged love, not punishment."

Other religions have similar patriarchal, autocratic beliefs regarding the inferior status of children and the adults' right to use punishment when disciplining children. When speaking to parents across the spectrum of cultural/religious/familial beliefs, I ask these two questions:

"When you disciplined your toddler, what did you teach her?" and

"Could there have been a better way?"

THE REAL MEANING OF DISCIPLINE

We need to remind ourselves that this little toddler is a vulnerable, impressionable person, newly emerged from the cocoon of babyhood. Harsh methods of control should not be on the list of disciplinary options, no matter how exhausting and infuriating their behaviour may be.

The words, **discipline** and **punishment** are not synonymous; discipline is derived from the word **disciple** – someone who is taught, guided and socialised. Essentially, effective discipline means learning from the consequences of choices. The parent puts the firm boundaries in place and then gives the child age-appropriate choices. These choices will involve consequences, which the consistent parent is able to enforce.

Below is a tabulation of the differences between discipline and punishment:

PUNISHMENT			DISCIPLINE		
Character-istics	Underlying message to child	Likely result	Character-istics	Underlying message to child	Likely results
Emphasis on power of personal authority.	*Do what I say because I say so.*	Rebellion. Desire for revenge. Lack of self-discipline. Sneakiness. Irresponsibil-ity.	Emphasis on reality of the social order.	*I trust you to learn to respect the rights of others.*	Cooperation. Respect for self and others. Self-discipline. Reality.
Rarely related to act; arbitrary.	*I'll show you! You deserve what you're getting!*	Resentment. Desire for revenge. Fear. Confusion. Rebellion.	Logically related to the misbehaviour: sensible.	*I trust you to make respon-sible choices.*	Learning from experi-ence.
Implies moral judgement.	*You're bad! You're not acceptable.*	Feelings of hurt, guilt. Desire to get even.	Treats person with dignity; separates deed from doer.	*You are a worthwhile person.*	Senses he or she is acceptable even though behaviour is not.
Emphasis on past behav-iour.	*You'll never learn. I can never count on you.*	Feels unacceptable. Can't make good deci-sions.	Concerned with present and future behaviour.	*You are able to take car of yourself.*	Becomes self-evaluating, self-directing.

PUNISHMENT			DISCIPLINE		
Character-istics	Underlying message to child	Likely result	Character-istics	Underlying message to child	Likely re-sults
Threats of disrespect, violence or loss of love, either open or concealed.	*You'd better shape up! No child of mine would do a thing like that!*	Fear. Rebellion. Guilt feelings. Desire to 'get back.'	Voice communi-cates respect and goodwill.	*I don't like what you are doing, but I still love you.*	Feels secure about parents' love and support.
Demands compliance.	*Your prefer-ences don't matter. You can't be trusted to make wise decisions.*	Rebellion. Defiant compliance.	Presents choice.	*You are capable of deciding.*	Responsible decisions. Increased resourceful-ness.

Taken from *Systematic Training for Effective Parenting Manual*: Don Dinkmeyer and Gary D McKay

> "Punishment is a very ineffective method of discipline … for punishment, strangely enough, often has the effect of teaching the child to behave in exactly the opposite way from the way we want him to behave! Many parents use punishment simply because no one has ever taught them better ways of disciplining their children."
>
> Dr Fitzhugh Dodson: How to Parent

Why is effective discipline of toddlers so difficult?

- We don't understand the toddler developmental challenges.
- As a result, we have totally unrealistic expectations.
- We say *no* too much. We also shout, threaten, use negative labels and you-language, so they become immune to our methods of behaviour management.
- We don't really mean what we say, so they very quickly learn how to manipulate.
- We then convince ourselves that nothing other than a smack will work, and then become really inconsistent, wavering between an over-permissive approach of allowing sthe toddler to push the limits too far, and then totally losing patience and becoming autocratic and harsh.
- We forget that toddlers have a very different sense of time. They are not constantly

time-watching (and having to go for body stress release therapy!) They need fair warning and patient understanding of their view of the world.

For all the above reasons – and many more – downward spirals begin during this stage, sowing the seeds for future discipline problems.

How negative cycles develop

Negative toddler behaviour

↓

Over-harsh parental reaction

↓

Shouting, too many *nos*, threatening, smacking

↓

Parent-toddler power struggles

↓

Toddler develops negative self-image
"I am bad and naughty"

↓

Escalation of negative toddler behaviour

↓

Ever-harsher parental reactions

↓

Poor parent-child relationship

↓

Ongoing discipline problem

So herein lies the challenge for parents of toddlers. Future discipline problems can be minimized if they are handled properly in the beginning, using appropriate and effective management skills.

Let there be no confusion here: **Toddlers definitely do need boundaries – these provide the predictability, routine and structure so vital for their feelings of physical and emotional safety and containment.**

VERY IMPORTANT TODDLER DISCIPLINE TIPS

- **Avoid absolute orders.** These will only press the buttons of power struggles.
- **Give them appropriate choices.** Though these should always be within boundaries, by giving them choices, you encourage their sense of autonomy and need for control (the key to their successful accomplishment of the main developmental challenge).
- **Give them adequate warning.** "We can have ten more swings and then we need to go to the car."
- **Mean what you say!** Don't tell them you will put their toys in the trash-bin for the garbage collector to take away unless you really will. And that would definitely be an over-harsh consequence for a toddler to handle!
- **Little people need few rules, but they need to know that these rules will be upheld.** Eventually, no matter how well you handle your toddler, you will need to put your effective discipline skills to the test. In the next four chapters we will thoroughly test the efficacy of the following model, by looking at many of the most common toddler behavioural problems, starting with a thorough review of the concepts of choices and consequences.

What effective discipline involves

- **Make the rule/expectation very clear.** "We do not hurt children when we play with them."
- **Get into the I-language habit.** This is usually before the 'rule' is actually broken. "I can see you are very frustrated because you want the same toy as Luci has."
- **Give a clear choice – with a consequence attached.** "If you push Luci again, you will have to come and sit next to Mommy until you can play nicely."
- **Follow through with the consequence.** "I see you have chosen to come and sit next to me." (Emphasise that she made the choice.)

This is a crucial part of the learning process where the toddler learns that it was not an arbitrarily given and harsh 'punishment', but rather a choice she made after being told the 'rule' and what the consequence of breaking the rule would be.

In the case of toddlers who are impulsive, emotionally immature and often spontaneously aggressive, a parent may have to be extremely vigilant and act very quickly when unacceptable behaviour erupts. "That was not a nice way to behave. Jessie is very sad. Now you need to come and sit with me until you can play nicely again."

Ultimately, parents of toddlers need to react firmly but calmly. Assertively, but not aggressively. Remember the example of the sandbag in the bomb blast? Meeting aggression with aggression will only detonate an even more powerful explosion. Once a consequence has been imposed, remain closely connected, both emotionally and physically.

> "The act of disciplining a child can be a frustrating one. However, at the outset it needs to be stressed that discipline means **education**. Discipline is essentially programmed guidance that helps people to develop internal self-control, self-direction and efficiency. If it is to work, discipline requires mutual respect and trust. On the other hand, punishment requires external control over a person by force and coercion. Punishing agents seldom respect or trust the one punished."
>
> Brian G Gilmartin: *The Case Against Spanking* in
> *How to talk so kids wil listen and listen so kids will talk*, A Faber and E Mazlish

SUMMARY OF CHAPTER 9

- Most parents will find reasons and justifications for 'just a little smack'.
- The problems with smacking:
    - Poor role-modelling. Toddlers learn to imitate adult behaviour.
    - Exacerbates aggression – already a problem for toddlers who have no ability to channel negative feelings other than via aggressive behaviour.
    - Toddlers may also be reacting to unmet needs and then get unfairly 'punished'.
    - Smacking a toddler can easily become like a drug-habit: you have to increase the dose to get the required outcome.
    - Causes escalation of power struggles and feelings of resentment and humiliation. Does not model a respectful way to deal with unacceptable behaviour.
- Why do parents smack?
    - It relieves stress and tension.
    - It was done to them, so they are repeating patterns.
    - They truly believe, "It did me no harm."
    - If you don't show a child who is in control, you will have chaos and anarchy.
    - For religious reasons.
- The real meaning of discipline:
    - To teach, guide and socialise. It is not synonymous with punishment. It essentially means learning from the consequences of appropriate choices.
- Toddler discipline tips:
    - Avoid absolute orders.
    - Give choices.
    - Allow adequate time.
    - Have few rules.
    - Mean what you say.

- Model for toddler discipline:
  - Make the rule/expectation clear.
  - Get into the *I-language* habit.
  - Give a clear choice – with a possible consequence.
  - Follow through with the consequence.
  - Stay close by and give the assurance of emotional containment.

10

Toddler-type consequences

THE ART OF THINKING ON YOUR FEET!

Whenever the issue of toddler discipline is raised in workshops and discussion groups, the responses to the mention of avoiding smacking in favour of giving choices that involve consequences go something like this …

"Yes, but how do I remain calm and collected in the face of an enraged toddler who has another child's hair in his vice-like grip, refusing to let go. What is the choice here?"

or,

"Yes, that's all very well if you are dealing with an older, more rational and verbal child, but you simply can't reason with a totally irrational two-year-old!"

or,

"Yes, but a quick smack seems so much more effective, because there just isn't time for all that I-language stuff and making deals."

You will notice that there are a lot of, 'yes … buts'! So let's tackle this thorny issue as thoroughly as possible.

Reminder

Regarding the basic principles of a Choice/Consequence approach to discipline:

- The essence of effective discipline is that learning takes place when the consequences of choices have to be faced.
- Learning from consequences leads to resilience and self-discipline.
- It is non-punitive and respectful.
- It enhances positive self-esteem.
- Most importantly in the case of toddlers, it does not exacerbate power struggles, and it encourages autonomy and a sense of independence that are core developmental challenges for the toddler stage.

Advantages of giving choices
- Reduces conflict, resentment and defensiveness towards parents.
- Each choice provides the child with an opportunity to take responsibility and exert some control over her life.
- For parents, choices help to establish parameters and limits. It is the parents who decide the option and present the alternatives that they are prepared to permit.
- Choices always have a built-in limit. One can't have everything.

Some problems with choices
- They must be age and situation specific. Toddlers are only able to deal with limited and specific choices, for example, "Which jersey would you like to wear, the red one or the blue one?"
- Often toddlers do not like the choices given. They may become angrier, more rebellious and say very negative things. Parents can accept these negative feelings and reflect the toddler's unhappiness: "I can see this makes you very cross," but then simultaneously re-assert the choice.
- Giving a choice should never be about the lesser of two evils, "Do you want to go to your room or have a smack?"
- Choices need to be fair, reasonable and logically related to the behaviour in question.

PUTTING ALL THIS INTO PRACTICE

When a baby is moving towards toddlerhood, parents need to remain very close to the child and direct her towards safe and acceptable behaviour. The toddler who grabs a chunk of a playmate's hair, needs to be told very firmly, "No, that is not a nice thing to do. We don't pull hair."

Do not shout or yell. **Never** pull her hair to show her how it feels. **Never** smack her for this behaviour. Make it clear by your very firm and adamant tone that you are not impressed, but **don't** use you-language, as in, "You nasty bully!" Firmly pull her fingers away from the hair and empathize with 'the victim': "That really hurts. Jamie did a very nasty thing." Then remove Jamie to a quiet spot so that she can calm down. When she has done so, give her something else to do to channel her frustration, "Let's rather throw and catch the bean-bags." This way, Jamie will be learning a far more valuable lesson than if you smacked and shouted at her.

Create distractions
Initially, choices can be in the form of distractions. If your two-year-old son is totally fascinated by plugs and knobs (and seems hypnotised by all the taboo things in the house), avoid saying, "No," to everything to which he is attracted. Rather try a very

firm, "That will hurt you, but you can play with your box of plugs in the TV room." An inquisitive and creative toddler will become totally frustrated if his fixation with plugs and knobs is constantly thwarted. Find a box and fill it with old gadgets and appliances (all safe, of course). You could even keep some of the smaller and more portable ones in a bag so that he can be occupied in the car, while waiting for the doctor etc. At this early stage, the toddler is a bundle of curiosity and enthusiasm. The world is new and exciting and she is mobile, so can actually reach all these amazing things. She is learning to exert her own will by saying, "No," and throwing tantrums. As a result, she needs firm containment and boundaries need to be set.

Child-proofing the environment, having realistic expectations, and staying calmly yet firmly connected will all go a long way during the transition to toddlerhood.

A rule for this stage

For every 'no' you have to say, try giving a choice of two positives. "You can't play with knives, but you can choose one of these spoons." "We don't pull the plants out of Granny's garden, but we can get the watering can to water them or pull the weeds out of the lawn. Let's go and see what we can do to help."

Remember that saying, "No," and shouting less will mean that when we really have to make it known that a toddler's behaviour is not okay, our firm, and possibly raised voice, will be enough to draw attention and act as a deterrent.

MORE ADVANCED CHOICES

The developing toddler will soon be able to make sense of simple choices:

"When the toys are packed away, we can go and play in the garden. If you don't help me pack away your toys, we won't go out and play." And this is where it all begins to go horribly pear-shaped ... the toddler refuses and sits stubbornly watching you, while you put away the toys. Do this calmly, saying, "Oh dear, I see you have chosen not to play outside." And then remain consistent, but calm.

If you don't ...

This is normally the point in the process when most parents 'lose the plot'. The toddler throws a fit (as only toddlers can!), the parent becomes angry and a power struggle ensues. Then one of two possibilities occurs:

The parent regresses to that autocratic, punitive 'other parent' that lurks in the background and finds it very difficult to keep control, resulting in a smack. This sorts it all out – or so it may seem ...

or,

The parent buckles under the pressure, "I just can't stand this kind of thing when I'm tired at the end of a busy day," and gives in to the furious toddler. "Oh alright then, let's go out and play for a while, but *next time* you refuse to put away your toys, there will be no playing in the garden."

If you do …

If you can stick to the choice you gave, your toddler will be learning a very powerful life-lesson.

- I was given a choice.
- I then made a choice.
- The boundaries remained consistently in place. My parents really mean it when they give me a choice.
- My parents are capable of enforcing the consequence of my choices.
- Therefore I have a choice regarding the consequence. I could have helped tidy up and then we could have played in the garden. Next time it will be easier to just tidy away the toys!

Of course this process takes a while to internalise. But this will occur as the child grows and develops – and it will be most effective if the parents have integrated the important principles of effective discipline into their own repertoire of skills and reactions. This is essentially a gradual development of the brain processes:

- There are rules.
- I choose to break the rules.
- I therefore also choose the consequences for breaking the rules.
- However, there are always opportunities to make better choices.
- And therefore more positive consequences.
- So, it's actually all up to me and the choices that I make!

"It is not our abilities that make us who we are Harry, but the choices we make."
Dumbledore to Harry Potter, from J.K Rowling's book, *Chamber of Secrets*

There can be non-negotiable rules at any age or stage

The most important aspect of the implementation of effective discipline is the parent's ability to establish firm, clear and consistent age-appropriate boundaries. It must be re-membered that we all feel more secure when we know what is expected of us, and the younger the child, the more they need the safety of predictable rules and limits. Even as they push and test these limits, they need them to remain firmly and calmly in place.

At each age and stage, children need to understand that there are non-negotiable rules in their family/playgroup/school etc. "In this house we do not shout." "When we are angry, we never break things." "It is not acceptable to hurt people." As children mature, the non-negotiable rules will change.

SETTING THE PARAMETERS WITHIN WHICH CHOICES CAN BE MADE

The essential aspect of giving choices is that a parameter is set, and the choices are given within these parameters.

a. "We need to bath every night. Do you want to finish your puzzle or bath first and then finish the puzzle?"

b. "We have to find some toys for all the children to play with. Do you want to leave all your toys in the playroom or put some special toys away?"

c. "We do not smack people. If you don't want to play nicely then you will have to come and sit next to me for a while."

d. "We do not eat sweets while we are shopping. If you go on shouting and yelling then you won't be able to come shopping with me next time."

e. "You may have ten more swings. If you fight about leaving the park, we won't come back tomorrow."

Let's see how the above examples may play out:

a. Tessa chooses to go on with her puzzle, then kicks up a fuss when the bath is ready. "You chose to finish your puzzle, now you need to come and bath." Pick her up firmly and take her to the bath. You can empathize with her, "I know you were having fun but we had a deal and you chose to finish the puzzle and then bath." If she goes on performing, try distracting her. Bubbles and water play soon do the trick. **Bottom line:** stay firm and calm. *Never* give in and allow extra time for more puzzle building.

b. Brendan decides to leave all his toys out, but then becomes very possessive when the friends arrive, not allowing anyone to touch any of his toys. "You decided to leave all your toys out, let's find some toys for everyone to share … or maybe I will have to decide. We either do that or perhaps you need to come and sit quietly with me while you think about it." **Bottom line:** Toddlers are irrational and egocentric and therefore find sharing very difficult. Be gently firm, enforcing a choice and a consequence.

c. Aimee, very frustrated, hits her playmate when she picks up Aimee's favourite doll. "I see you have chosen to come and sit with me for a while. We can then ask Caitlin to give your doll back. But we do not smack people." **Bottom line:** Try not to fall into the trap of over-reacting. Stay calmly firm and allow the consequence. Remember it is not a punishment, therefore does not have to be harsh or punitive.

d. Justin throws a fit at the checkout because he desperately wants a sweet. Get through the checkout as quickly as possible and stay calm, reminding him of the non-negotiable rule. "I know you'd love a sweetie. You may have some raisins or biltong. But if you go on yelling you will have to stay with Daddy next time I go shopping." Justin probably won't care, or hear. Calmly, take him home (that is, *you* stay calm, he probably won't!) When you need to shop again at a later stage, say, "We had a bad time with sweets last time. This time you need to stay with Dad." And then stick to it! **Bottom line:** Although it may be tempting to just forget what you said would happen if he chose to make a fuss, make a point of remembering, and very gently, yet firmly, remind him of this. The lesson learnt is that mom means what she says when she gives a choice.

e. Isabella had to be dragged, kicking and screaming, to the car after her allotted 'last ten swings'. "Isabella, we had a deal … now we can't come to the park tomorrow." When the usual playtime in the park is due on the next day: "I'm sorry we can't go to the park today, because we had a very bad time yesterday. We can try again tomorrow." **Bottom line:** Ignore the resultant temper tantrum. Empathise with the anger, but do not allow this to sway you into relenting – no matter how much easier this may be!

SOME RELATED ISSUES AROUND TODDLER CHOICES AND CONSEQUENCES

- Many parents, whether they are conscious of it or not, still view **discipline** and **punishment** as the same thing. They will therefore react with, "But just sitting with me after he's pulled his friend's hair is not a sufficient punishment." However, we must remember that a **consequence** means learning from a **choice**. A toddler who is isolated for a while (even if this is sitting next to Mom) is learning that, if he can't resist being aggressive, he will be removed from the play. We are **teaching**, not **punishing**.
- "But she really doesn't care," is another oft-repeated sentence I hear. Maybe not. The issue is not whether she cares or not. It is that she is learning that there are limits, and consequences for not adhering to these limits. Whether she cares or not it's irrelevant, this is the side effect of the autocratic approach to discipline: the child must *feel it* and show remorse. However, this is not the main aim of toddler discipline; feelings of remorse and regret will only come much later.
- Don't get caught in the 'defiance-trap'. When following through with toddler consequences, it is very common for the furious toddler to do exactly what he's been told not to do. "I see you've chosen to give your blocks to me," may be met with a toddler who then throws them *at* you! Many parents will then say, "Surely the defiance

deserves a good smack?" This may be a strong-willed toddler's way of showing his disappointment and fury at being forced into the consequence of his behaviour. **Do not retaliate**. Remain firmly in control. "I can see you are very cross, but you had a choice. It was very bad to throw your blocks at me. Now I will put them away until you are ready to stop throwing them."

• A good toddler consequence is the 'think-about-it-chair' or the quiet corner. *Note: not the 'naughty chair' or the punishment corner.* "You need to stop pushing Lucy or maybe you need a few minutes on the think-about-it-chair. If the behaviour still persists: "It seems you have chosen a few minutes on the chair," rather than, "That's it, you are a little bully! Now you need to go and sit on the naughty chair for five minutes."

• Time-out can also be a contentious issue for toddlers. They are still very little people and much of their unacceptable behaviour, while needing to be limited, is actually within the limits of normal toddler behaviour. A two-year-old having to leave the centre of play to sit quietly with a parent for a while, is time-out enough.

At this age, they are very scared and anxious about being locked in a room, so try not to do this. There have been TV programmes that advocate a minute for each year of the toddler's life. This is not necessary. At the toddler stage, 'time-out' can be just being taken to another room or out into the garden for a while. It really is a way for an out-of-control little person to be removed from a provocative situation in order to find emotional equilibrium. (More about serious temper tantrums later.)

Handled correctly at this stage, time-out (quite rightly) becomes the consequence of a choice made. It is when this is incorrectly used by an angry and retaliating parent that it merely acts to exacerbate power struggles. "Now get to your bedroom for five minutes," is likely to stir the fires of rebellion and rage. However, if it becomes a choice early in a discipline process, such as, "Either sit and eat properly with us or you may go to your room until you are ready to behave at the table," it is more likely to be viewed as the consequence of a reasonable choice. *Note: this example is for an older child.*

Another note on time-out

I have been asked the following question more times than I can remember: "But going to his bedroom is not serious enough. Besides, other parenting experts have told me that the child's bedroom should be a happy place and that the time-out place should be without fun or distractions." I am afraid that I then become somewhat flippant, saying something like, "Should it be the cellar or a dungeon?" "No," the confused parent normally answers, "but what about the toilet or bathroom?" The issue here is that time-out should be just that. Not a serious punishment in a harsh and unpleasant environment, but a chance to go and gain control of emotions and to learn that, when parents give a choice, they really do mean it. And that they are capable and assertive enough to ensure that the consequence of the choice is carried out.

A word on the issue of 'saying sorry'

So many adults will insist that a tiny tot, hardly even able to string a coherent sentence together, must 'say sorry' in order to gain re-admission into the toddler society. "You can stay on the think-about-it-chair until you are ready to say sorry," is the stock-in-trade sentence. However, the problems are countless:

- The toddler does not even have a developed conscience yet. This is only beginning to develop (in its immature state) by about the age of six or seven.
- It therefore means absolutely nothing! The amenable toddler may say it as a pro-grammed robot would. It is really just a 'get out of jail' phrase, with no meaning at all. Many adults continue with this habit during their lives: saying sorry, but with no real emotional connectedness to the word.
- As parents, it is necessary to role model the value of an apology but, for the toddler, this is a separate issue. They need to learn that, whether sorry or not, they will be re-

admitted to the group when the unacceptable behaviour stops, and that caring adults will assist them. Then, as a separate process (and part of developing emotional intelligence) they will need to learn the value of an apology – but they must really mean it. "Katy is so sad that she had her hair pulled, it would be very good to say sorry," or in the case where the toddler is not yet verbally proficient, "Katy, Megan is very sorry that she hurt you." **But try not to insist at this stage**. It will either lead to bigger power struggles, or to a robotic, knee-jerk response in order to get out of the consequence.

Using the 'countdown' method as a part of a consequence

"You need to put away your toys and if you have not done so by the time I count to five, I will have to put them away for a few days." The inherent problem with this is that it invites resistance – especially from the strong-willed ones. It's as if they think, "Let's see what happens when she gets to five." Many a proud parent will say to me, "Oh yes, I give choices: I count to five and, if it's not done, they know they'll get a good hiding. They have *chosen* this!" This is **not** the accurate meaning of effective choices and consequences.

Rather give a clear time-frame, for example: "We can go out to swim once the toys are put away." No threats or power-issues and no counting-down or dire warnings. Just a simple statement of what is expected before something desirable can take place.

And finally, in the case of toddlers, the consequence should be firm yet gentle. It should preferably be as immediate as possible; however, sometimes the consequence cannot take place immediately (for instance, at a crowded supermarket checkout). It may then be necessary to remain calm at the time, weathering the storm and dealing with the embarrassment. When you get home, say, "I felt very unhappy at the store. You need to sit quietly in your think-about-it-chair," or, "I don't think we will watch Barney yet. It was very upsetting when you made such a fuss. You can watch Barney later."

....

SUMMARY OF CHAPTER 10

- Allowing toddlers to begin learning from the consequences of choices is a vital aspect in learning to apply positive alternatives to smacking and other negative methods of discipline.
- Advantages of giving choices:
  - Reducing conflict, resentment and defensiveness.
  - Opportunities to feel in control of choices.
  - Parents provide the parameters/limits within which choices are made. This provides a sense of security.

- Choices also have problem areas:
  - They must be age and stage appropriate.
  - Parents need to be consistent and firm; toddlers may not like the choices.
  - They should never be the lesser of two evils.
  - They must be logically related to the behaviour.
- General issues when getting into the choice-consequence habit:
  - Try using distractions.
  - For every *no* try giving a choice of two *yes* options.
  - At each stage there should be non-negotiable rules.
  - Beware of being pulled into the defiance trap.
  - Consequences like the use of a 'think-about-it-chair' or a quiet corner are useful for toddlers.
  - Time-out should be carefully used in the case of toddlers. You are not looking for a severe punishment, but rather a consequence of a choice given and a chance to gain equilibrium.
  - The countdown method can provoke power struggles in strong-willed toddlers. Rather give toddlers a tangible rule, like: "The toys must be put away before we can watch Barney. If they are not tidied up, there won't be any Barney."

We have now reached the end of the first section by working systematically through the issues and the skills that ought to have provided you with the tools to be in a better position to effectively parent your toddlers. And particularly, to have a more realistic approach to the contentious issue of disciplining a toddler. I sincerely hope that you can now see that most of the negative behaviours which characterise this stage are, in fact, normal and in line with the developmental challenges with which a child of this age is supposed to cope in order to be emotionally equipped for the next stage – that of the pre-school child.

At this age, discipline should never be harsh and punitive. It is essential that parents provide clear and consistent boundaries for their toddlers, but the choices (and subsequent consequences) should be gentle and realistic. The aim is not to **punish** but to **teach**, and the essence of effective teaching is to learn from the consequences of mistakes. The most crucial part of an effective discipline process is the adult's reaction to the toddler's behaviour … and this is where the capable and mature adult learns to make positive choices.

It is therefore clear that so much of toddler behaviour is not intentional nor consciously negative and vindictive: they are simply doing what toddlers do!

The big four toddler issues

1. SLEEPING / 2. EATING / 3. POTTY-TRAINING / 4. TANTRUMS

This section, divided into four chapters, provides an overview of the most common toddler problem areas for parents. Consequently, I have entitled it *The Big Four Toddler Issues – Sleeping, Eating, Potty-training and Tantrums.* These issues cause most of the problems typical of the toddler stage, and yet they should never become serious discipline problems, especially the first three, which are physical issues. However, when not handled carefully at this stage, they can lead to many of the more serious problems in older children and teenagers.

Toddlers need firm, clear and consistent boundaries, but within these parental limits they need to feel that they have age-appropriate choices. These choices will encourage their autonomy and, hopefully, minimize power struggles.

11

Toddler issue 1: Sleeping

There is nothing more debilitating and energy sapping than broken sleep on an on-going basis. Parents expect this during the new baby stage, but patience wears very thin when it extends into the toddler stage. Or, worse still, when the baby develops a predictable sleep pattern, which then disintegrates as the toddler stage unfolds. For extremely good, sound advice on the establishment (and ongoing reinforcement) of calm and consistent sleep routines, I highly recommend the book by two of my Metz Press colleagues, Megan Faure and Ann Richardson, entitled *Sleep Sense – Simple Steps to a full night's sleep.* I would go as far as to say that this should be compulsory reading for every new parent, though it is not too late to go back to the basics when your toddler gives you hassles and headaches over sleep problems.

> *"Sleep Secret: Although you may have concerns about strategies to cure an unhealthy sleep habit, the truth is, if you start early with sleep coaching, by preventing sleep problems, you will most likely avoid ever having to implement strategies to cure undesirable sleep habits."*
> Megan Faure and Ann Richardson: *Sleep Sense*

PARENTS CREATE THE PROBLEMS

One of the most frequently stated sentences I have heard over the years is the one that goes something like this: "My son makes me sit with him until he falls asleep." There are many variations on that theme: "I have to pat Tessa until she is sound asleep," or, "I lie with Brent, in fact, I usually fall asleep too. As soon as I try to ease away from him, he starts yelling again. It's simply easier to stay with him," or, "Our lives have been on hold since Jenna was born. She won't let anyone else put her to bed," and so it goes on.

Can you pick up the common thread here?

- The toddler is calling the shots.
- The parent has **allowed** the habits to become entrenched.

- The parent has confused the issues of **going to sleep** (which is difficult to enforce without medication) and **time to be in bed** (whether the toddler falls asleep or not).

It is very important to take a long, hard look at how the habit has been formed. If a baby is never left to settle herself to sleep – always being rocked, patted or held until she falls asleep – of course this will be her primary sleep-association! Therefore, the first step towards establishing better sleep habits is to take responsibility for how the habit became entrenched and begin to make changes. Bear in mind though, that it is totally unrealistic to expect a two to three-year-old toddler, who cannot settle himself to sleep, to be 'cured' overnight, because the habit has probably developed over this period of time. What usually happens is that parents have not managed that initial transition from newborn baby with enormous needs (to be held, cuddled and fed on demand) to the older baby who begins to expect immediate gratification (and gets it from parents who continue to succumb to these demands). Suddenly, this baby who probably got used to falling asleep on the breast, or while being held closely and bottle-fed, becomes a very demanding toddler who still expects similar treatment!

The harassed parents are then faced with the consequences of their own earlier choices and begin to run out of patience. And this is usually where the biggest mistakes begin: sleep patterns develop into power-struggles and, unfortunately, punishment appears to be the only solution. "If you don't go back to your bed right now, I'll give you a smack," or, even worse, "If you are not asleep by the time I come back, I will take your new Pooh-bear away."

Never make 'falling asleep' into a discipline issue – rather focus on 'bedtime'

Remember that sleep is a biological necessity, although people need differing amounts and will also find unique ways to sooth and settle themselves into the most conducive ways to ease themselves towards that sleep. Different temperaments will also react to sleep patterns according to genetic predisposition. A lively, extrovert, highly active toddler will, in all likelihood, take longer to settle into sleep than a more docile, calm and introvert toddler. It becomes a matter of learning to understand your particular child's emotional and sensory needs. If a reactive, energetic toddler has been on the go all day and, when it is suddenly time to go to bed, takes longer to settle than the parents feel is necessary, power struggles emerge and sleep becomes a discipline issue. And this can quickly lead to unfortunate and escalating problems.

Toddlers, especially the strong-willed and more obstructive and defiant ones, very quickly realize that you cannot force them to fall asleep. When they realize this, the fun and games begin and they can stay awake for hours – just to show you who is boss!

Boundary setting and bedtime

While not allowing bedtime to become a war-zone, it is essential to establish firm, clear limits. However, the central issue should be that the boundary is **bedtime** – for example, "When we have put the teddies to bed, brushed teeth, had a story and a cuddle, then it is time to stay in bed." *Note: No mention of, "You must go to sleep."* In other words, if the little rebel wants to stay awake for hours, it's fine, as long as she stays in her bed while she stays awake!

As in the establishment of any effective rule or limit, parents must ensure that:

- They really mean what they say.
- They will follow through with the enforcement of the limit.
- They will not 'lose it' and become harsh and punitive.
- They will remain calmly consistent and very firm so that the toddler realizes this is non-negotiable and serious.

- They will not allow the boundary to be moved – not even by the most persistent and determined efforts on the part of the toddler.

Remember: It is the adult reaction to the toddler's behaviour that will determine the long-term behaviour of the child.

So, if you are firm and determined one day and then permissive and easily persuaded to move the limits the next, your toddler will learn to fight harder and longer – just in case this is one of your permissive days! Rather do not make rules that you cannot stick to.

THE IMPORTANCE OF ROUTINE AND STRUCTURE

This cannot be highlighted strongly enough. The younger the child, the more they gain their sense of security and emotional stability from the predictability of an established routine. As adults, we may thrive on spontaneous flexibility and lack of rigidity but, even the most free-thinking people will admit that they feel more secure when they have feelings of safe containment: there will be food for supper, a place to sleep tonight and hopefully, money in the bank tomorrow!

Because toddlers are in a developmental 'space' where they are learning so much every day (new skills, feelings of separate identity and, especially, the ability to develop autonomy and a sense of control), they desperately need to feel securely contained within a predictable routine, even while simultaneously fighting against adult-imposed restrictions.

Applying this to the issue of bedtime and sleep routines
- Establish a set routine leading up to bedtime. This should be a matter of slowly disconnecting from the stimulation of the day and working towards a calm and relaxing bedtime, in a sensorily gentle and sleep-inducing space.
- The routine itself should send the message: *we are moving closer to bedtime.* Therefore, do more or less the same things in the same order, for example:
  - Last bit of playtime in the garden or toy-corner.
  - Calm and relaxing bath.
  - Time for supper.
  - Quiet playtime. Puzzles, putting dolls/teddies to bed. (No TV or DVDs.)
  - Toilet or nappy changing.
  - Last drink from cup or bottle.
  - Story and cuddle time.
- Now its bedtime. The night-light is on, cuddly toys are in bed and perhaps a quiet Mozart CD is playing. The parents exit gently but are firm about leaving, although the toddler does know that they are close by.

But what about boundary-pushing?

This is where the bad habits of the baby-stage may come to bite you! The only way to instil your determination into your toddler is by remaining **very calm** but **very firm**. She must learn that you really do mean what you say. So, each time she tries to get out of her bed with pleas of, "Me thirsty," or, "scared," or, "sad," simply take her straight back to bed. Remember all the skills we have already discussed:

- Allow feelings: "I can see you would like to stay with mommy and me, but it is bedtime now."
- Use I-language: "I'm beginning to feel very cross and I don't want to shout, so into bed **now**."
- Give appropriate choices: "I need you to stay in bed now. If you get out again I will have to take you straight back."
- Allow the consequence: "Now I'm very cross – back to bed **right now!**"

Points to remember

- Never make a discipline issue out of a physical one. Therefore, it is not the **sleep** but the **bedtime** that is the rule/limit.
- Avoid power-struggles. You will end up with a no-win situation: a sobbing toddler and a desperate, angry (and perhaps guilty) parent, and you will probably end up giving in and staying with your toddler. This is a win for the toddler but very bad news for your effectiveness as a parent.
- You are training your toddler to know that bedtime is definite, but she has choices regarding how and when to fall asleep.
- When you really mean it (and stick to it), your toddler will be less likely to fight against the boundaries that will become a source of predictable security to her.
- Remember that we are talking about very young children here. The consequence for an older child would be age-appropriately more stringent. For example: "If you get out of bed one more time, we will only have a very short story tomorrow night," and this would then have to be remembered when bedtime comes the following night. "You chose to only have a very short story tonight because we had a bad time last night at bedtime."

What about exceptions?

These will always occur because life throws curved balls and unforeseen circumstances arise:

- Grandparents visit from overseas, so children sleep in different beds.
- Toddlers get ill and mom and dad take turns to sit with the sick child to ease them into sleep.
- Dad/mom goes away on a business trip, so the little one has a 'treat' and is allowed to sleep in mom/dad's place.

The rule of thumb with situations such as these is:

- Try not to change habits too drastically. Rather do not allow sleeping in a parent's bed if possible, as this just throws you back a few steps – and will make re-establishment of the usual habit more difficult. A case to mention is when parents get divorced. Many a parent has said to me, "But he felt so insecure at the beginning, and I loved having him with me, but now it's a real problem to get him back to his own bed again." So rather never allow the precedent to be set.
- When there are exceptions (the child is ill or granny has the use of the child's room), get back to the old routine as quickly as possible when things revert to normal. "I know you slept in our room while Nanna was here, but now she's gone home and you need to go back to your own bed."
- Another problem that can become entrenched regarding bedtime habits is when the baby/toddler in the bed becomes an 'excuse' not to reconnect with a partner. This is frequently a presenting problem in relationship counselling. One partner will say, "Jeremy is still in our bed, and he's just turned three. Desiree makes every excuse to keep him there. So now I'm sleeping in the spare room, it's causing enormous tension between us and will lead to a split." Poor Jeremy has well and truly become 'piggy-in-the-middle' and has become accustomed to his right to usurp his father in the marital bed. Not a healthy situation and very unfair on three-year-old Jeremy. Desiree doesn't acknowledge that it is being used as an excuse to avoid dealing with the real, deeper issues, "But Jeremy becomes so distressed when we try to get him into his own bed. I just can't take the tears and tantrums. It's easier this way, but only for now. Sooner or later he'll want to be in his own bed." But sadly for Jeremy, his dad may have left by then and he'll be another divorce statistic.

The 'musical bed' scenario

"My two-year-old is fine about going to bed. He co-operates so well; we have always insisted that he goes to bed in his own bed/cot and, from the outset, he has been able to fall asleep on his own. But now he has suddenly begun to wake up at night and wants to come to our bed."

This is a variation on the sleep theme, and a difficult one, because if parents are really honest about it, it is usually a matter of having allowed a habit of another kind to develop. That is, it is just easier to allow the toddler to creep into bed with you in the middle of the night … especially in winter. Then the 'Musical Beds' game begins, with one or other parent ending up in the toddler's bed or the spare room, just for the sake of a peaceful night's sleep! All the same rules and issues apply as in the getting-to-bed routine:

- Do not allow bad habits to develop.
- Realise that you have a role to play in future behaviour. However, if you and your partner do not have a problem with the behaviour/habit, then there is no issue. That

is, until you begin to feel stressed about the behaviour, but then you need to take responsibility for allowing it to develop in the first place!

- **Calm but firm** is the mantra to recite.

Points to ponder regarding night-time waking

- They do not wake up on purpose. Therefore, your toddler is definitely not being intentionally naughty.
- They wake for a reason/need. The quicker the need is met (a drink of milk or water, a cuddle of reassurance, a gentle yet firm reinforcement of the need to stay in bed), the quicker the toddler will settle back to sleep.
- Toddlers have dreams and nightmares. They have fears and anxieties and these may manifest at night. Do not make the mistake of telling your little one, while he is clinging to you for reassurance, that there is nothing to be scared of. Rather remember the importance of empathy, gently soothe him and say, "I am right here with you," and *then* reassure him, "There is nothing to be afraid of; the light is on, Mommy and Daddy are right here." Your calm firmness will be all he needs.
- Avoid inconsistency: being available and understanding one night, and angry and impatient the next. This will only confuse the toddler and will not help with effective resolution of sleep-related problems.
- In cases where the bedtime routine is dictated by over-dependence on parental presence, it must be remembered that every time the toddler has to settle back to sleep during the night, the same routine will be expected. If you rock your toddler to sleep at bedtime you will, in all likelihood, be expected to go through this ritual during the night too!

The use of a 'transitional' bed

A final point on the issue of sleep problems:

If your toddler is securely entrenched in your bed, and your efforts at getting her to sleep in her own bed have failed dismally (and even the promise of a beautiful, designer Barbie or Bob the Builder bedroom has not succeeded in enticing your determined toddler into that bed), then maybe an effort at desensitisation may be the answer. That is, a process of slowly and firmly getting your toddler out of your bed and into his own.

It will seldom work to suddenly insist that she move from the security of your bed to her own bed in a separate room. So, rather begin with, for example, a camp-mattress kept under your bed, which you use as a means to get the little one out of *your* bed, but still allow the security of being close to you. You will then need to be very firm about the fact that sleeping in your bed is now non-negotiable. Once you have made the move from your bed to toddler-mattress, then the move to toddler-bedroom should be easier.

The mattress is also a better option for night-time waking than allowing incursions into your bed. In our family, that mattress was called 'The Nest' – a safe and secure night-time spot that provided reassurance without disturbing exhausted parents unnecessarily!

In this way, you will be gently assisting your toddler to break habits that, for whatever reason, you have allowed her to develop. The secret of success will be in the way in which you, the parents, remain calmly, gently, and firmly focussed on creating better sleeping habits for you and your toddler.

> "Sleep Secret: Allowing your toddler to sleep next to your bed is a step in the direction of sleep independence."
>
> Megan Faure and Ann Richardson: Sleep Sense

12

Toddler issue 2: Eating

Feeding a baby/toddler/child has become an integral part of being a 'good' parent – especially a good mother. Mothering and feeding are often seen almost synonymously. It clearly begins in infancy, when a contented baby is one with a tummy full of milk. Mothers who battle to breast-feed immediately feel that they have in some way let their baby down and failed as mothers. This extends to toddlerhood when that thriving baby becomes a strong-willed toddler who adamantly refuses every tasty morsel her desperate parents tempt her with, which causes her anxious parents to immediately feel that they are in some way failing their child. In other words, if they were capable parents, they could at least get their two-year-old to eat a balanced diet!

Similar to the issue of sleeping, toddlers very quickly realize that this is an area of their little toddler lives that they can control totally. Maybe Mom and Dad are big and forceful enough to buckle them up in the car seat (or remove them from a Toddler Group when they begin to behave aggressively), but there is an enormous feeling of power when a two-year-old begins to realize that no one can force them to eat! Even when an adamant dad insists on putting the yucky vegetables into a toddler's mouth, there is an enormous feeling of power when this horrible mush can simply be spat out onto the floor. And a defiant toddler may simply refuse to open his mouth at all!

WE CREATE THE PROBLEMS

As in the case of sleeping, calm, gradual and consistent eating-patterns will unfold as the baby grows into toddlerhood (and then childhood) if adults would only try to avoid those escalating power struggles caused by angry, harsh and punitive reactions:

"If you don't eat your porridge we can't go to Granny for tea."

"By the time I count to three you must have swallowed your mashed potatoes."

"You naughty, messy child! How could you spit out your chicken?"

"You can stay in your high-chair until you've eaten all your lunch."

On the other hand, you could spend your days making the food they like, and then they shake their heads stubbornly, saying, "No, not hungry," or refuse to even *try* the special toddler-type spaghetti bolognaise you came home early to prepare. Your frustration reaches boiling point and you say something totally inappropriate like, "I have slaved over a hot stove when I might as well have been lying at the pool with my new book." Your two-year-old could not care less about your wasted time and energy. Remember that they are still totally egocentric; they only care about themselves!

The other scenario is the patient, loving, over-anxious parent who turns mealtimes into an hour-long playtime/therapy session – with entertainment laid on as an added extra! The toddler is coerced and cajoled into taking mouthfuls in return for a parent's joyous hand clapping, dancing and various other contortions. The toddler is mesmerized into eating without actually realising it! But how can a parent keep this up?

Once again, the amenable toddler will more than likely oblige … at least some of the time. The problem is that the more temperamentally challenging toddlers will very quickly realize that eating is very important to adults!

Never make eating a discipline issue

Eating is a biological necessity. No child who has access to healthy food will ever die of hunger. But when toddlers, especially the stubborn, strong-willed ones, realize what power they can exert by simply refusing to eat, the scene is set for an ongoing ding-dong battle of wills. And the more adults exert pressure via threats, bribes and punishment, the more the power-struggle is exacerbated; a very unfortunate situation for all concerned.

Just for a few minutes, put yourself in your toddler's shoes. Imagine yourself being happily lost in a new book you were given. The last thing you feel like doing right now is eating. Your partner shouts for you to come to lunch and reluctantly you go, but see that he has made fried chips and sausage, which is the *last* thing you want. He tells you how ungrateful you are – after all he has gone to all this trouble. You fiddle with the food and he tells you that if you don't eat everything on your plate, he won't take you to the movie as arranged earlier. He then puts some chips on your fork and tells you to open your mouth and stop being so stubborn. You totally lose it at this stage, picking up your plate and dumping all the greasy food into the bin. You then go to your room in a temper and go back to reading your book, while your very irate partner yells at you, slams the door and goes out for the rest of the day!

Maybe it's ridiculous to draw analogies between a toddler's stubborn refusal to eat and an adult's situation – but they cannot be forced to eat any more than we can. And they will react very similarly (in a toddler-type manner) if they are disciplined for not wanting to eat!

BOUNDARY SETTING AND EATING

Try never to make mealtimes into an unhappy and stressful power struggle. Nothing positive comes from forcing a toddler to swallow when the child is hell-bent on not succumbing to the pressure. Eating should be a normal, pleasant, sociable time for toddler and family.

Therefore, while you can't force the toddler to **eat**, you can establish healthy boundaries around the business of mealtimes. From as early as possible, create a routine and predictable structure around mealtimes. In many modern families, the problem is that mealtimes are not calm and structured. Adults are in such a rush to fit too much into a day that meals become a frenzy of quick bites here and there. For example, a sandwich in the car while driving, breakfast while standing or checking emails, TV suppers, etc. So toddlers do not learn to associate eating with a calm time to sit, connect and concentrate on the meal.

Toddlers will begin to learn that, at certain times and with adequate warning, like, "When Daddy gets home we will have supper," the family sits together to eat. Whether they eat everything on their plate is not the issue; the issue is that there is a time for eating, so if the toddler does not feel like eating that is fine – but the consequence will then be that he may have to wait until the next mealtime.

But what about boundary-pushing?

As in the case of all other behaviours, parents need to take a careful look at how behaviours have been formed. When toddlers push the limits regarding eating habits, it is usually because parents have been inconsistent; wavering between permissiveness and punitive harshness. One day allowing the child to eat a banana while playing in the garden and the next insisting that she sit at the table and eat all her vegetables ... and totally losing it when she refuses. Fortunately toddlers are still very impressionable and easily moulded, even the most challenging of them. But they need to know that their parents really mean what they say, and are capable of remaining calmly, firmly consistent.

Remember these skills?

- Allow feelings: "I can see you do not want to eat those carrots."
- Use I-language: "I will be very happy if you try just one carrot-stick."
- Give a choice: "You need to eat a bit of carrot before you have any ice-cream. But the ice-cream can wait until you feel ready to eat the carrot. You can decide when you are ready."
- Allow the consequence: "I see you have chosen to have ice-cream later. That's fine. We can keep the carrots for when you are ready."

We will talk about temper outbursts later.

Points to remember regarding food and eating

- Be as calm and matter-of-fact as possible.
- You are not forcing eating, but you are putting certain limits in place. For example, it is fine not to eat the vegetables, but then the consequence is no biscuits or cake later. The toddler soon learns that she is making the choice.
- Do not become over-anxious: running around all day offering tempting food because you are so worried that your toddler will fade away! He will very quickly realize exactly how he can get to you and will manipulate you in order to get you to jump to his every culinary whim!

Picture this scenario: A ten-year-old who holds his parents to ransom at mealtimes:

> Tom: "Oh yuck, you know I hate cottage pie. I want pizza. You promised I could have pizza today."
>
> Dad: "Tom, you eat what your mother has cooked – we are not ordering pizza today."
>
> Tom: "I won't eat that junk. I'll just go to bed hungry. You never care about what I want."
>
> Mom: "Oh Tom, don't talk like that. Okay, just this once, I'll phone the Pizza House. What kind do you want?"
>
> *Tom smiles smugly, thinking, "It's so easy to get Mom to feel sorry for me." Dad looks furious, and this will surely lead to a heated parental 'debate' later.*

- Do give a choice if it is possible. "I am about to make lunch. Do you want a chicken sandwich or fish fingers?"
- Remember that toddlers have very small tummies. A dietician gave excellent advice at a seminar I attended. She said that portions should be more or less the size of a fist. Look at your two-year-old's tiny fist, and give small portions relative to this.
- They have to feel they have *some* control. Give them variety and make it attractive. A few carrot sticks, sliced apple, slices of cheese, a cherry tomato, small pieces of chicken or shredded lettuce. Let her taste, touch and leave what is not acceptable.
- Do not be over-anxious about mess (within reason) because if your toddler is learning to use a small spoon and fork, there *will* be spills so make allowance for this. If her urge to touch, experiment and be creative can be incorporated into eating, you will have a happy toddler who is also eating, even if you have to get out the mop to clean

up the mashed butternut and the peas that missed her mouth! Being over-controlling and too much of a perfectionist will only lead to anxiety and avoidance, as mealtimes become a stressful and unhappy experience.

- Some toddlers are texture-sensitive. They hate the texture of some foods or try to avoid anything lumpy. This can be a result of over-processing the food or not mashing it enough. Slowly introduce different textures. A good hint is to encourage the child just to put the food into their mouth – even if they spit it out once it is there!
- Then there is also the fact that growth happens in spurts. At times the toddler will eat eagerly and at others, it may decline. Their bodies will tell them when to eat more.

Many parents have anxiously said, "I'm so worried. My toddler just never eats a full meal. He's going to get really ill if he goes on like this." My advice is usually as follows:

- Relax and remember that no child will die if food is available.
- Make sure he has a good vitamin supplement.
- Ensure there are no 'junk-food' fill-ups.
- Then, without drawing attention to it, make notes over a two-week period. You will be surprised at what he *does* eat – as long as you are not supplementing with sweet-treats or crisps! He may not be eating the typical three-meals-a-day that make parents and grandparents feel happy, but he is probably getting all the nutrients he needs for his age and level of growth.

Some food-related pitfalls

When a child wails pitifully, "I'm hungry daddy/mommy," shortly after a battle of wills at mealtime when the child refused to eat a thing, it touches a nerve with the frustrated parent, who had handled it by saying, "That's fine, but then there's nothing to eat until supper-time." To avoid the pitfall of giving in to the starving child, it would have been better to say something like: "That's fine, but I will put your lunch under a cover, so you can sit at the table when you're hungry. Or you can have an apple or a banana later." When the furious toddler then says, "No, I don't want those, I want biscuits. I'm really hungry," simply say, "If you are hungry you can have your lunch or the fruit, but there are no biscuits." End of story!

The other anguished question is often: "But if she had no supper, what happens if she's hungry in the night?" Well, she will certainly learn that it's better to eat supper! However, she could be given a cup of milk, maybe even a half a banana if the issue of hunger is disturbing the whole family, and she should be fine until the morning. If she then refuses supper the next night though (possibly remembering that a midnight snack was rather pleasant), be very firm, "There will be no snacks in the night." If she then wakes up and wants bananas and milk, just give a few sips of milk and stick to the 'deal', even if you have a bad night. She will soon learn to eat supper – or she will eat a very good breakfast!

Here's another food dilemma that sometimes raises its head: "I gave a choice. He chose the fish fingers rather than the chicken. When I gave him the fish, he yelled that he wanted the chicken. What do I do?" You may want to ram the chicken down his throat, but stay calm, and simply say: "You chose the fish. There is no chicken. If you don't want the fish fingers I'll keep them for later. You can have some raisins or a pear."

(See Chapter 14 for the handling of the temper tantrum that will probably erupt at this stage!)

As with sleeping, it can be seen that the cardinal issue is not to make eating into an enormous power struggle ending in threats and over-harsh punitive reactions. Establishing sensible, age-appropriate boundaries around meal times, and allowing toddlers to feel that they do have some choice within these boundaries, should avoid long-term problems.

13

Toddler issue 3: Potty-training

Now we really are hitting a central toddler control issue! This is truly where the battle of wills can come to a conflagration! The parents' need to get rid of the nappies and to move beyond the unpleasant toileting aspect of babyhood is in direct conflict with the toddler's powerful inner drive towards control and autonomy. This is the famous psycho-therapist, Sigmund Freud's famous 'anal stage' when, according to Freud, the child's healthy psychological development hinges on how the toilet training progresses.

I don't believe there is any other stage which is as crucial for the delicate parental balancing act – between the child's need to feel in control, and the parents' need to set limits without over-pressuring and an over-volatile reaction. Once again, as in the case of sleeping and eating, going to the toilet should be a purely physical necessity, which should ideally develop calmly and gradually; a normal and natural part of childhood development.

Why does it become such a war-zone for so many toddlers and their parents?

• The myths of old wives' tales: I well remember the confusion I felt when my very sweet and well-meaning mother-in-law proudly told me that her children were potty-trained at eight months! I later realized (when common sense prevailed) that it was actually their mother who was 'trained'. After a meal, she would dutifully get out the little potty and hold the obliging baby's bottom on it. The baby's reflexes reacted, so the child seemed 'trained'. I now know better; the muscles and connected brain-process take at least two years to develop to the point where the toddler can:
  – realize that there is a need to go to the toilet.
  – control the bowel or bladder muscles until he gets to the toilet.
  – get there, take off the necessary clothing, sit on the toilet/potty and relieve himself.

This process begins with the toddler wetting or soiling himself and beginning to realize that he has some control over this. Only later will he be able to stop the process until he has got to the toilet. Until this stage, the process of elimination has been an entirely involuntary one.

- Add to the equation the toddler's need for control of her own body. She very quickly learns that the matter of nappies/potties and toilets is extremely important to her anxious parents. They begin to remind, coax, beg, cajole and reward her. But then they also become frustrated, irritated, angry and even disgusted. Therefore, the message the toddler receives is that this is exactly where **she** can call the tune and the scene is set for a powerful battle, especially in the case of the challenging and strong-willed toddler. Whether it happens consciously or subconsciously, the little person quickly learns that this is yet another issue that is very difficult for parents to enforce.

  A toddler (resisting the pressure being exerted by these controlling, stressed adults) will either refuse point-blank to sit on the potty and then go on to 'do the business' soon afterwards, or will comply and sit on the potty and then begin to learn the powerful art of manipulation that psychologists call 'passive-aggressive' behaviour. So, he will sit on the toilet like a good boy, do nothing, and then go out into the garden and do it there! It's as if they are saying, "You can't force me to do things your way. I can choose to do these things in my own way and my own time."

- The insidiousness of these downward spirals then begins to take a firm hold. The infuriated parents beg, coax, threaten, and finally, punish. The equally furious toddler (not wanting to lose control of this very individual and personal choice) digs her psychological heels in even more, and the scene is well and truly set for an unfortunate, and escalating, conflict of wills where there is no winner. The only outcome will be a lose-lose one. On the toddler's side of the fence is an angry, sad, resentful little person with a diminished sense of autonomy and a dented self-image, while on the parents' side, there are feelings of failure, despair, anger and guilt. This is not a happy outcome for something that is such a natural, physical necessity. However, the reality is that too many adults put the proverbial spanner in the works by triggering unnecessary power struggles with their over-zealous attempts to hasten the process.

SO WHAT IS THE CORRECT WAY?

Simply put: by tuning in to your toddler's developmental 'clock' and focusing calmly and empathetically on her temperament and her readiness to find ways to feel in control of her needs, while simultaneously learning the necessary coping skills. For most toddlers, at around two to two-and-a-half years old, the first step occurs naturally when parents notice that nappies are dry at times, which means that a level of bladder control is developing. Training pants and pull-up nappies are an excellent aid to assist the toddler in becoming aware of the occurrence of bladder and bowel action, and introducing the toilet via special potties, toddler toilet-seats and little steps to help reach the toilet, are all moves in a positive direction.

From then on, the more calm and gentle the approach, the better.

- *Avoid absolute orders.* "You must sit on your potty before we can go out." These only trigger power struggles.
- *Make tentative suggestions.* "Should we try going to the toilet before we go out?" Or, "Do we need to go to the loo now or should we have some juice first?" This approach is so important for avoidance of future problems.
- *Use descriptive praise.* "That was very good. You managed to go to your potty all by yourself. Well done!"
- *Do not overact to mistakes.* "Oh dear, I see there was an accident. Let's get the toilet paper and then change your pants."
- *Beware of rewards!* Rewards can be as ineffective as punishment. Both place the emphasis on external issues and present an opportunity for manipulation. "If you go to the toilet like a good boy, you can have four sweets." The easier toddler may respond well to this and co-operate, however, beware those switched-on, bright, 'manipulators'. I have an indelible picture of one of my own toddlers, clearly bursting to go to the toilet, but breathlessly saying, "Want lots of sweets." In other words, this little horror had already learnt to bargain and four sweets just weren't enough anymore!

The issue of toilet training should really be a non-fussy process of appropriate, descriptive praise, balanced with equally appropriate, non-punitive disapproval of failure to co-operate.

Other relevant issues

- Toddlers do regress. A child may have been toilet trained relatively easily, only to regress to wetting and soiling later. Often this may be related to a traumatic event, for example, the birth of a sibling (see Chapter 16). The best approach is to handle it with understanding and empathy, but a measure of calm firmness. It may be the toddler's subconscious way of trying to get attention by reverting to being a baby again. Beware of saying things like, "Don't be such a baby," as this is probably *exactly* what she is aiming for! Rather say firmly, "Oh dear, I see there's been an accident. We need to clean this up and fetch another pair of panties." However, be sure to give her plenty of positive attention in other ways, as in: "Come let's play a game while the baby's asleep. It's so nice to have time with my big girl." This will reinforce her role as the 'non-baby' and decrease her need to get attention by regressing.
- Obviously, night-time control takes longer to develop. As I have already stated, relieving oneself is a complicated brain-process: the full bladder or bowel sends a message to the brain which relays a message to the relevant muscles to hold on until the toilet is available. Once this has been achieved, another message is sent, saying that release-action is in order! Now add to this the fact that the little person is sound asleep, which makes the whole procedure more complicated: the brain must wake the toddler up *as*

well as everything else! In some children this can take years rather than months. So leave the night nappy for longer in order to avoid unnecessary stress. Only when the nappy is dry (or almost dry) remove it, and remember to place a waterproof sheet over the mattress during the trial-and error-phase.

- There are also other night-time issues. During the toilet-training regime, it is important to gradually limit the amount of liquid intake. Obviously, a toddler who is drinking copious amounts just before bedtime, and during the night, will have a fuller bladder, so will need to urinate more frequently. However, as in the case with all the already-mentioned toddler scenarios, try to avoid power struggles over this. Do not suddenly, and harshly, withdraw the bedtime bottle, as this will only lead to stressful bedtimes. Rather continue using a night-time nappy while gradually limiting the liquid intake, and *then* deal with the nappy issue. *One baby step at a time* is a good mantra for parents of toddlers.

  A frequently used method of ensuring a dry bed in the morning, is the habit of parents 'lifting' the toddler before they go to bed and encouraging him to use the potty. However, this is more likely to create further problems, rather than solutions, because:
  − the sleeping child becomes irate at being so unceremoniously woken up and then refuses to co-operate. Now you have a toddler whose sleep pattern has been broken and you have to re-settle him!
  − you are actually delaying the child's natural process of learning to wake up when his brain receives the *you-need-the-toilet* message. I believe it's simply more helpful to postpone the relinquishment of the night nappy.
- Genetic factors. If either parent, or a close relation (for example, a grandparent) had a problem with bed-wetting, your child may have inherited this tendency. It may then be advisable to take the older child for a paediatric check-up but, at the toddler stage, it may be premature to become too anxious, as it is very unusual for such a young child to be able to gain sufficient control to be dry at night.
- Boys normally take longer to toilet train than girls, and are also only ready for the whole training process a bit later too.

POTTY-TRAINING AS A BOUNDARY ISSUE

If adults have sufficient knowledge and realistic expectations of this stage of development, potty or toilet training should not easily become a discipline issue:

- A toddler should **never** be punished for having an 'accident' – either during the day or at night.
- The parents' role in boundary setting is to create the age-appropriate parameters and give choices: "We need to go to the toilet before we can go to the park." Remain calm and leave it up to the toddler. No coercion, just gentle reminders. If the toddler

refuses, then calmly state, "Oh dear, I see we are not going to the park today." Your toddler will soon learn that you don't really mind whether you go or not, but she will be upset and, if you resist the power struggles, will soon realize that it is up to her.

- Toddlers will push the limits. Remember that your reaction to the boundary testing will be the determinant as to how future issues develop. Your child will soon realize that your positive reaction to co-operative behaviour is far preferable to your some-what detached, matter-of-fact reaction to defiance and testing. "It is not nice to wee on the carpet. Now we need to get hot water and a sponge to clean it up. I am not a happy mommy right now." Clearly, you should only use this reaction once you have seen that your toddler can actually go to the toilet quite successfully. During the trial and error learning stage, accidents will be par for the course!

- Beware of your over-harsh reactions at this stage. The more challenging the toddler's temperament, the more difficult potty training can be. A more obstructive and defiant little 'tyrant' will go to any lengths to show you who is in control here, and a serious medical condition – encopresis – can develop as a result of a negative power struggle. In this case, the toddler **will not** sit on the toilet or potty to do a bowel movement and nothing the parent does will entice him to do so. He withholds and, as a result, becomes constipated and, when he eventually has to go, it is painful and unpleasant, resulting in a vicious cycle, which leads to the need for medical intervention (enemas, softening remedies) and an escalating battle of wills. Usually, the root cause was an over-controlling parent and an equally controlling toddler who quickly learnt that this was something he could 'win', but at an enormous emotional and physical cost.

- This takes us back to good old Sigmund Freud's observations, as well as the well-used phrase: 'She's such an anal person – a real control-freak!' In real terms, this basically means a person with a strong personality who learnt at the toddler stage that she could get the better of situations by controlling them totally.

- Don't allow your toddler to get you under his little thumb! As with sleeping and eating, parents recite phrases such as, "She **makes** me put her nappy on before she will have a bowel movement." Or, "He throws a tantrum if I put his nappy on at night, but if I don't, the whole bed is soaked in the morning." Once your toddler has success-fully managed to be trained during the day, do **not** allow her to call the shots. You do not **have** to put her nappy on her: that is not negotiable. Either she goes back into nappies completely or she has no daytime nappies. If she chooses not to go to the potty or toilet but, to 'spite' you, does it in the garden or behind the couch, deal with it very firmly, showing her that you are not at all pleased, but that she will not get undue attention for it either. Remember that if you do something even once (putting on a nappy because she demands it), she will continue to demand this until she learns that there is a parameter and that you will not allow her to **make** you do anything that is not helpful in the longer term.

Finally, it is encouraging to be reminded that no child whose development has proceeded relatively normally, will go to Grade 1 in nappies! But this same child may very possibly carry the emotional scars of over-punitive toilet training if the parents did not learn the importance of the realistic expectations of a toddler.

14

Toddler issue 4: Tantrums

It should be very clear by now that much of what is viewed as 'naughty, 'rebellious' and 'defiant' in toddler behaviour, is actually normal for a child at that stage of development. Hopefully it is also clear that many future discipline problems have their origins at the toddler stage. This is largely due to the unfortunate reality that the physical functions of sleeping, eating and toilet training are too often turned into major disciplinary power struggles. In this way, the seeds for ongoing parent-child conflict are sown, and the sad fact is that this could be avoided by a combination of knowledge of child development, realistic expectations and effective parenting skills.

No overview of toddler behaviour can be considered to be complete without a mention of the behaviour that is a central feature of this stage of child development.

TODDLER TANTRUMS

This behaviour is so typical of this stage that one could quite reliably say that *toddlers* and *tantrums* are synonymous. I have mentioned this aspect of toddler behaviour in relation to many of the examples that have occurred in the preceding chapters. However, I feel it is necessary to devote a dedicated section to this most distressing of behaviours, which has no doubt been the main reason behind describing this developmental stage as '**The Terrible Twos**'. To fully understand the reasons behind these irrational outbursts, it is necessary to look at the world through the eyes of a two-year-old.

My name is Joshua and I have just had my second birthday. I felt very important and excited because Mom and Dad gave me a shiny red scooter. I wanted to ride it in the street outside our house because my friend, Kyle, does that. Dad said I couldn't because I am not old enough, and the only reason Kyle can do it is because he is four. I felt so disappointed and mad, so I threw my new scooter down and started crying loudly. My mom said I was naughty because my scooter got scratched, so she pulled me by my arm and told me to sit on the naughty chair. I felt even angrier then so I just kept getting off it. Then my dad shouted at me and said that he would cancel my party. But I knew he wouldn't, because he always says things like that, but then he changes his mind.

I did have my party and it was fun. I had a Superman cake, sweets and cool drinks. But then my cousin Jessica tried to ride my new scooter and no one even asked me, she just took it. I screamed at her to give it back, but she wouldn't, so I pulled her and she fell off. Then everyone was calling me names and my mom smacked me. That was it; I just yelled and cried and then I got locked in my room. So that made me madder and I kicked the door until they let me out. I couldn't tell them how I felt because I'm just beginning to learn proper sentences. I just felt so angry and my party was spoiled because Jessica went and took my new scooter.

In order to understand the toddler's world, the first step is for adults to comprehend how frustrating it must be to experience strong feelings, yet have no way to express these other than to throw a tantrum. The next step is to develop appropriate coping strategies. I refer back to the analogy of the 'feeling egg', and highlight the fact that when the toddler is in a state of emotional disequilibrium (a tantrum), it is useless to try reasoning and explaining. He simply will not hear you, and his rage will usually escalate. The only way to help him cope with his overwhelming feelings is for capable, calm and empathic adults to help him contain his feelings:

- Say as little as possible but what is said needs to be gentle and calming.
- If he will allow it, hold him firmly (but gently) until you feel the tension in his body easing. Toddlers feel very insecure and afraid when their emotions overwhelm them – it is very scary for a two-year-old to 'lose it' so completely. (Think of yourself: It is not exactly a good feeling when emotions have got the better of you either, and you're an adult!)
- Try to 'catch' the feelings before they escalate to the stage where the toddler's behaviour has reached the point of no return. If it *has* reached that point (some toddlers can go from calm and co-operative to totally out of control in a matter of seconds), then **never** try to reason or cajole. Talk as little as possible and stay close by to ensure he doesn't injure himself. Do not put a two-year-old in a room and close the door. This is a desperate little person who has lost control of his very overwhelming feelings.
- Try distraction, but time this very carefully. It works best when 'the eye of the storm' has passed over. Sit quietly alongside the child and talk or sing softly about something other than the issue that led to the outburst. You could also bring out his favourite book and look at it together. Any one of these suggestions may help the toddler to come out of the tantrum.
- Of course, it is by now very clear that the adult should never react harshly or punitively. (Remember the sandbag in the bomb blast – Chapter 6). The toddler must get a very clear message that the feeling is always acceptable, but the behaviour is often not. So, he is not having the negative feelings repressed, but he *is* being taught that the behaviour he is choosing to express these feelings may not be acceptable. An

example would be: "I know you do not want Jessica to play with your new scooter, but we do not push people over when we are cross with them." Follow this up with a choice: "Shall we put your scooter away until after the party, or will you let Jessica have a quick turn? We can count to ten and then it will be your turn."

– Never, ever, give in to the toddler's tantrums. This will only reinforce in the toddler that throwing a fit can be effective.
– Never forget the impact of over-control when it comes to eating, sleeping and toilet training.
– Finally, and probably most importantly, never be tempted to give your out-of-control toddler a smack for his tantrum-throwing behaviour. *I will really give you something to scream about* may be the sort of threat that is tempting for an exhausted parent trying to cope with this irrational behaviour, but it will obviously teach the toddler nothing about how to express himself more acceptably in the future. Another common reaction is to tell the toddler that there is nothing to be so upset about or to ask too many questions. Unhelpful comments like, "Stop being such a baby!" and, "Why are you crying?" are totally lost on the toddler who is in a state of total emotional disequilibrium and hasn't the slightest idea why he feels so upset!

A few words about the obstructive, defiant and very challenging toddler

There is no doubt that some children are born with a genetic blueprint that predisposes them to being stubborn and obstinate. As we have already discussed, if they are well managed, these traits can be channelled into all the positive ones that they possess – enthusiasm, energy and determination. And remember to avoid labelling these more difficult toddlers too easily. Rather deal firmly and assertively with the **behaviour**.

No matter how impossible your toddler may appear to be, bear in mind that this is a very small person who is learning how to behave acceptably by the way he sees you react to him. You, the mature adult, hold the key as to how his childish attempts to gain control will gradually evolve.

Finally, if you sincerely feel that you have done everything in your power to help your toddler to cope better, and *nothing* seems to be working, seek professional help. A thorough assessment by a paediatrician is always a positive step. However, it is never advisable to begin labelling a challenging toddler as 'hyperactive'. For one thing, it is difficult to diagnose a two-year-old and for another, it is all too easy to find solace in labels. Many a 'highly active' toddler has been over-hastily labelled as 'hyperactive' just because he is hard to handle.

There is no doubt that clinical conditions such as ADD (Attention Deficit Disorder) and ADHD (Attention Deficit Hyperactive Disorder) definitely do exist, but even in these cases, the most important part of the management process is effective behaviour management by the adults in the child's life. This, coupled with very firm limits on stimulation (restrictions on the amount and type of TV and DVDs watched, as well as rules regarding sugary foodstuffs), will almost certainly result in more manageable behaviour.

The more determined the toddler, the more essential it is that parents put firm, clear and consistent boundaries in place. These little fighters need to know that, even when they rage against the limits, their parents are capable of calmly maintaining them. This ability to provide a secure container will provide the stability and predictability so essential for the toddler's healthy personality development.

In other words, a two-year-old's temper tantrums are perfectly normal. They have strong feelings, but not the skills to express them. Just as a baby learns the labels for objects by having them taught to her, so a toddler will learn the labels for feelings by having empathic parents who are capable of teaching her the correct words (and then gradually, also appropriate behaviours) to express these emotions. Toddlers need to feel that they have control over their lives. This is how they develop a sense of identity and independence. When parents use punitive, harsh methods of over-control, this conflicts directly with the toddler's inner drive, and throwing a tantrum is the only way this little person can let the world know just exactly how mad he feels. If he is then punished for this, he will never learn the vital skill of expressing his feelings in socially acceptable ways.

The 'good' ones

It is also very important to bear in mind that some of the more amenable and easy-going toddlers may learn that it is not acceptable to express these negative feelings. They then develop other ways of coping with their toddler emotions; for example, they may repress 'unacceptable' feelings or develop an over-strict conscience. These are the 'good children' who do not express their true feelings out of fear of the consequences. They are then in danger of developing what the psychologist Alice Miller called the "false self". This essentially means that they learn that they need to be just as their parents want them to be in order to be loved and accepted. This can then lead to depression, rebellion and serious identity confusion in later stages of personality development. Of course, there *are* those children who have a naturally laid-back and relaxed temperament that don't feel the need to express very strong feelings, but it is those who have never been *allowed* to express their true feelings (for fear of over-harsh parental reaction) who will almost certainly present emotional problems later.

I believe that the central, most important, step in the development of emotional intelligence is to be in touch with one's feelings and to possess effective ways of expressing them. And there is no doubt that one of the most vital keys to future success in life is to have large doses of EQ (emotional quotient). There used to be enormous emphasis on the child's IQ (intelligence quotient), where parents were desperate to know their child's IQ score (as assessed by educational psychologists), and would be heard to boast at dinner parties: "We are so proud of David. He was tested and his IQ is in the superior range!" While this may be helpful for teachers to assess whether he is over or under-achieving, it would be a far greater 'feather in parental caps' if the child were to be assessed at an advanced level of emotional intelligence. And, although it may sound simplistic, a very positive foundation can be laid if adults are capable of effectively handling the challenge of their toddler's tantrums!

Summary of the big four toddler issues

SLEEPING, EATING, POTTY-TRAINING AND TANTRUMS

- In the case of the first three (eating, sleeping and potty-training), the most vital 'rule' to remember is that these are all physical/biological needs. All humans have to sleep, eat and eliminate waste products!

- Many of the problems that arise around these functions are caused by parental over-control. Just at the time when toddlers are trying to achieve autonomy, parents desperately want to exert control and socialise their toddlers as quickly as possible.

- The strong-willed, determined toddler will fight that much harder, and destructive power struggles will result, which has a very negative impact on the parent-child relationship.

- No amount of coercion and harsh methods will force a defiant toddler to fall asleep, eat or go to the toilet. The issue here is that the boundary-setting needs to be clear and enforceable. There need to be consistent and structured routines around these areas. For example:
  - Being (and staying) in bed.
  - Sitting at the table at a certain time.
  - Choosing to go to the toilet, rather than wear a nappy.

- Be as consistent as possible. Exceptions do occur but do not deviate from the routine more than is absolutely necessary, and, if you allow occasional exceptions to the rule, revert to the usual routine as quickly as possible.

- Allow age-appropriate choices within the security of firm limits. "It is time to stay in bed. You can have your special light on and two teddies. Let's choose them and put them to bed first." "When this puzzle is finished it will be lunch-time. Do you want me to put honey or jam on your toast?" "We are going to the shop. Do you want to go on your potty before we go or shall we put your nappy back on?" When your toddler can't (or won't) choose or co-operate, then simply make the choice for her, but always stick to the basic rule.

- In the case of tantrums, always remember that your calm and containing reaction is the key. A toddler tantrum is an 'emotional blown fuse'. They do not have the skills to express their negative feelings yet, so they 'blow'. Slowly helping then to learn that they are allowed to have the feelings – but need to learn more acceptable behaviour – is the central key to future emotional intelligence.

I feel that it is appropriate to repeat an earlier quote:

"Emotional Intelligence is the master aptitude, a capacity that profoundly affects all other abilities, either facilitating them or in interfering with them."

Daniel Goleman: *Emotional Intelligence*

15

Separation

EASING YOUR TODDLER FROM BABYHOOD TO PRE-SCHOOL

Toddlerhood is a transitional stage. At the one end of the spectrum is the total dependence of babyhood, and at the other is the relative freedom and independence of childhood. By then, the toddler has emerged from the cocoon of babyhood and has learnt to walk, talk, eat unaided, play co-operatively, share (sometimes!) … the list goes on and on. Most importantly, the pre-school child will hopefully have developed a sense of identity and assertiveness. The defiant 'nos' of the two-year-old, the uncontrollable tantrums when thwarted and the inability to resolve conflicts will have been refined, and the socialisation process will be developing positively. A key aspect of how positive this process will actually *be* is the manner in which the important adults in the child's life handle separation.

An intricate balance

From the moment the umbilical cord is cut, your baby will never be totally dependent on you again! Newborns do not yet have any understanding of their separateness. This is a gradual process that needs gentle handling and encouragement. A baby learns that her needs will be met, even if it means waiting for a while. The toddler learns the power of his own will to control his needs and demands. This is all an integral, and necessary, part of learning to stand on his own wobbly toddler feet. As is true of any transitional process, there are adjustment challenges, and a great deal of ambivalence and regression. One minute this determined little person is dead-set on going it alone: "Me do it," (said with total commitment to the challenge of putting on a tee-shirt) can be followed by a clinging, insecure, crying little person a few minutes later when it's time for parents to leave him with his child-minder while they go to an appointment.

This is what the separation process is all about – being allowed to cling like a needy baby one minute, while being praised for managing a task all on his own the next. Effective, capable parents have a firm grasp of the skills needed to achieve the intricate balance in this very delicate, and developmentally intricate, process.

Another factor in this crucial balancing act is the parents' own ambivalence. The longing for peace, space and the reclamation of a semblance of an adult identity, while simultaneously feeling lost and abandoned when children seem to be doing almost too well without constant parental supervision.

"I felt devastated when Jeremy and I returned from our glorious weekend away (the first since Amelia was born) only to be told by my parents that she didn't ask for us once! *And* she just went on playing with her toys when we arrived home after rushing back from our mini holiday as quickly as possible."

This is true ambivalence. We want them to cope without us, yet also pine for us at the same time!

THE INFLUENCE OF TEMPERAMENT IN SEPARATION

Some children just seem to be born with an innate sense of confidence and resilience. They go easily into new situations, relate happily to others and separation seems to take place as naturally as blinking and sneezing! Others are more cautious and clingy. They need time to 'test the waters' and weigh up the risks in new situations. They need to take things a little slower and separations should be handled with empathic sensitivity.

Usually toddlers waiver between the two extremes. So, one day they seem confident and capable, and the next, insecure and clingy. This is a sure sign that the characteristic ambivalence of this stage is manifesting itself.

However, there is a childhood temperament that can be classified as extremely anxious/shy. This needs a longer discussion, as this temperament type is very often mis-handled right from the start.

The shy/anxious toddler

In Chapter 5, we looked at the influence of temperament in understanding what influences toddler behaviour, and that learning to manage a child's basic temperament is possibly the key to all future parent-child problems. I have often highlighted the management of the more determined, strong-willed toddlers, while the shy and anxious toddler is often overlooked. This is possibly because they are so much easier than the typical, tantrum-throwing toddlers. The problems inherent in this temperament type often only manifest much later (as they tend to bottle up and avoid adult attention), unless their anxiety leads to fears, clinginess and a general inability to separate happily.

Often, when a toddler shows signs of shyness, a parent will identify with this: "I know how she feels. I was such a shy child too." But then the identification with the problem become over-developed and, in a well-meant attempt to help the toddler overcome the shyness, the parent will, unfortunately, try to overcompensate. This usually takes the form of finding ways to put the toddler in social situations in order to help her develop resilience and therefore overcome her shyness. The poor, clingy, shy little mite is booked into Toddler Workshops, Toddler Gym and taken to play-dates and birthday parties. Unknowingly, and usually subconsciously, the toddler's anxiety triggers the parent's deep-seated anxiety (which the toddler inherited from this parent in the first place!) and an ongoing cycle of feeding each other's anxious temperaments is set in motion. This often leads to the toddler's anxiety escalating and the parent, instead of seeking help for her/his own anxiety, begins a process of ongoing professional help for the child – even eventually resorting to anti-anxiety medication.

A word of caution here: I am not stating that professional help and medication are not necessary at times; they certainly are. But the 'first prize' should always be to try finding parent-effectiveness skills before exploring the other options.

Suggestions for handling an anxious/shy toddler

- *Learn to understand the temperamental needs* of this child.
- *Never force, push or pressurise* the toddler.
- *Try not to compare* the child to more outgoing and confident toddlers.
- *Avoid negative labelling and comparisons*: "Your friend Emily goes to playgroup all alone, why can't you?" Toddlers are unique individuals, each with special needs and abilities. Learn to handle **your** toddler, according to his/her special needs and temperament type, without comparisons.
- *Move slowly.* If your toddler plays happily at home and there is no need to send her to a playgroup, then let her play at home. Begin to slowly help her develop social skills by having one playmate at a time.
- *Social activities should be introduced gradually*, with someone the child has a secure attachment to available for reassurance and a sense of security.
- *Never, ever leave a toddler without saying goodbye.* Many a well-meaning parent has said, "But he was playing so happily, I thought it better that I quickly sneaked out." (Just imagine, for a minute, how you would feel if you were a shy person. Your husband takes you to a business dinner and you don't know anyone. He sees you talking to some people, so decides to quickly sneak out to his office over the road to check his emails. After a few minutes of chatting, you feel a bit anxious and go looking for him. You feel panicky when you can't find him and very angry and resentful when he explains later, saying: "But you were chatting so happily to the other wives." Will his behaviour help you feel less anxious and shy in the future?)
- *Verbalise feelings.* As in the case of the tantrum-throwing toddler, it is really important to help the anxious toddler understand that his feelings are perfectly acceptable, and to learn the labels for his feelings. "I can see that you don't want me to leave you because you feel shy," or, "It is so scary to go to a new playgroup," or, "Amy feels

very shy but she had a lovely time. Thank you." This approach is far more likely to help a toddler feel that:

– it is okay to feel the way he does, and

– he won't be forced into anxiety-provoking situations too quickly.

- *Remember the famous 'feeling egg'.* When anxiety is too high, the equilibrium is unbalanced and nothing worthwhile is learnt. Saying to a shy, anxious toddler, "There's nothing to be scared of" or, "Stop being such a baby, I'm only going shopping," or, "Don't be so silly. You know you love playing at Amy's house," or, "If you don't say 'thank you' to Joshua's mom right now I'll take away your new truck when we get home," will only exacerbate the toddler's innate sense of anxiety and shyness. These kinds of remarks do not help the toddler develop effective coping skills for managing a genetically-given temperament. He will feel punished for the way he is, totally misunderstood, and the anxiety will continue. And no-one can thrive physically or emotionally when in a perennial state of anxiety.

- Separation anxiety will only become worse. It is a surprising contradiction to a parent when they realize that the very problem that they are genuinely attempting to help the toddler cope with (by exposing him to social situations that are challenging), is actually being made worse by the very way in which they are choosing to deal with it. The fact is: *a shy toddler needs to be allowed to cling and be accepted just the way he is,* in order for him to feel secure enough to gradually learn to become a well-managed, shy child. This usually means a child who has not been made to feel that it is bad to feel shy and anxious. On the contrary, he has parents who have understood – and fully accepted – that he has a tendency to be shy/ anxious, and they have managed this via effective parenting skills. In so doing, their child has also learnt positive coping skills. This is the positive result of intelligent and empathic parenting.

SECURITY OBJECTS

Almost every parent of an older child will remember the days of babyhood and toddlerhood, when dummies, 'blankies', teddies and bottles were totally indispensable. Even though all four of my 'toddlers' are now grown up, I vividly remember harrowing moments when 'blankies' were misplaced and bedtime became a traumatic and heartbreaking experience while we were desperately searching for a temporary replacement. I also recall making a determined effort to 'give the dummy to the fairies' in the brave light of day, only to end up consoling a sobbing wreck of a two-year-old at 10pm – eventually despatching a long-suffering dad to the all-night pharmacy to find a replacement in order to get some peaceful sleep! As with all the other toddler issues, the best rule of thumb is to take it slowly. **Never** arbitrarily remove a security object. For example, many a parent has decided that the second birthday is cut-off point: "No more dummies or bottles," and, "It is time to throw away the shrunken, filthy remnants of that baby blanket." If you do this too hastily it will only lead to increased anxiety at a time when the toddler desperately needs the security of familiar objects, because so much else in their lives is stressful and demanding.

Of course, walking around all day sucking a dummy or bottle is not advisable either, and 'blankies' often seem to go hand-in-hand with dummy or thumb sucking as well. The 'trick' is to begin to introduce gentle 'rules', like, "We do not take a dummy when we go shopping," or, "Your bottle is only for when you have milk at bedtime." This is how your toddler begins to learn that her security objects are not available every hour of the day, but will be there in times of need.

Don't compare

It is important never to ridicule or compare, as in: "You are such a baby. Matthew doesn't take his teddy to playgroup." This sort of labelling will only succeed in lowering self-esteem. It will certainly not help to reduce anxiety or assist with the separation process. If your toddler needs to put his 'blankie' in his bag for playgroup, let him do so. He may never need it, but just knowing it is there may be an enormous source of comfort to him. Remember that a two-year-old is still very close to babyhood and should never be expected to behave like a 'big boy' because he definitely is not one!

As adults, we all have our 'security crutches': cups of tea, cigarettes, a glass of wine, a hair appointment, a game of golf, and these all help us cope when life gets stressful. So let that little two-year-old have his – there is plenty of time to gradually wean him off them before he leaves to get married!

The effective parent will see the value of security objects, especially during the toddler stage. This parent will be able to gently encourage less and less dependence on this special 'thing' and will be able to help the child wean herself off it, mainly by working towards a cut-off point or boundary, and then being able to firmly and consistently stick to the 'deal'.

GOING BACK TO WORK

Leaving babies and toddlers in the care of others

There is the natural process of separation, which takes place over the years of childhood and leads to the freedom and independence of young adulthood. Then there is the matter of a more 'forced' separation when a primary caregiver is faced with the very difficult question of: "When is the best time to return to work?"

This is such a difficult question to answer as it involves so many variables. Many mothers today have to (out of pure economic necessity), return to work soon after a baby's birth.

This subject is a whole book in itself. In fact, the 'guru' of baby and child development in the UK, Penelope Leach, has written a book called *Children First: What society must do – and is not doing – for children today*, which addresses the whole politically-loaded issue of day-care, crèches and Educare Centres. However, this is not the central issue of my book, suffice to say that there is no 'magic age' when separation is ideal. It will nearly always be a highly emotionally painful process, for parents and child.

It is very important that babies have the benefit of the full-time care of their mothers for as long as is possible. This primary bonding is of enormous psychological importance. The baby is then given an optimal chance of forming as secure an attachment as possible. And a secure maternal attachment definitely lays a foundation for future feelings of security and emotional safety, which are such vital ingredients for future separation experiences.

> **The more closely and securely the baby bonds with a primary caregiver, the more likely they are to cope with separation later.**

Therefore, spend as long as possible with your baby before returning to work, and obviously take great care when choosing alternate care for your baby.

Some guidelines for alternate care

- Choose very carefully and trust your gut-feel. Ask as many questions as you need to.
- When you are leaving a baby, it is better to look at home-based care first, such as having a nanny in your home (on condition that she is well-trained and has very reliable references). Of course an extended family member, if available, is an excellent option, or even a well-recommended day-mother who cares for no more than six babies and toddlers. A crèche/Educare Centre is usually too big, and the ratio of babies/toddlers to adult caregivers too high. Babies and toddlers under two need as close to one-on-one adult care as possible.
- Before returning to work, ensure that you have acclimatised the baby/toddler to the new environment/routine. Do a few 'dry runs', so even though you are not yet back at work, practise the routine exactly as it will be when you do go. This will help with any separation issues … the child's and yours!
- In cases where there is enormous doubt, sadness, resentment etc, regarding returning to work, a very important step towards positive acceptance is to find a good counsellor or therapist with whom to share your feelings. Even tiny babies can pick up the emotional vibes very quickly, and there is no doubt that these unresolved feelings could hinder the process of healthy and positive separation.

Separation and the older toddler

This also opens up an enormous area of concern. Questions like:

"When should I send my two-year-old to playgroup?"

"My 18-month-old is bored at home and needs the company of other toddlers."

"Will it be a disadvantage if I only send my child to playgroup at three?"

"Will my toddler be able to cope better in Grade 1 if she is enrolled in a stimulation programme now? She's just had her first birthday."

Once again, there are some important issues and guidelines here:

• Young children are seldom bored. We project how we would feel if we had to spend all day exploring a garden, chasing butterflies, emptying cupboards, messing with mashed potatoes and creating shapes with play dough. This is all very stimulating and exciting to a toddler as it is how they begin to learn so many important concepts.

While you chop carrots, measure flour, pour out noodles or tidy a cupboard, there is so much a toddler can learn about shapes, colours, textures, size and outcomes. This can never be boring to a two-year-old.

- If you are fortunate enough to be able to stay at home, relish this precious time with your child. Do not rush him off to playgroups too quickly, rather let him first form a secure attachment with a caring and loving primary caregiver. This safe and stable foundation will be the most positive factor in his ability to separate later. This means that the first step is a very firm and secure attachment, followed by the second step, which is the ability to feel confident that other attachments will also be safe. Overall, this results in a less stressful separation process.

- If possible, separate gradually. It is really good if you are in a position to begin the process of 'formal' separation by starting with the type of situation where you stay with your toddler. This will assist her to let go gently (with you nearby for reassurance and security). When she needs to go into a more formal set-up, it is often usual for a parent to be allowed to stay for the first morning, and then gradually leave the toddler for longer periods, until she is able to remain for the duration of the playgroup.

- When you need to leave your toddler, do so gently but very firmly: "I see you are not happy for me to go, but I must go to work now," and then **leave**. No lingering, regretful 'good byes', no turning back for 'one last kiss' and (error of all errors) allowing the child's sadness and/or anger to allow you to change your plans. "I just could not go through with it. She was heart-broken when I said goodbye, so I just phoned and cancelled my facial – I couldn't bear the fuss and anguish." A very silly decision, and one that will only lead to future manipulation. After all, if Mom stayed with me because I cried and made a fuss, then this is what I must do to make her stay with me! This will lead to ongoing separation issues, which eventually spill over into unnecessary discipline problems. In other words, the toddler's resistance to early attempts at separation will lead to bigger problems and resultant anger and frustration for the irritated parent. This unfortunate sequence of events then leads to escalating cycles of separation difficulties.

Separation anxiety is normal

It is important to note that there is a developmentally normal stage when most babies go through a stage of separation anxiety. This is usually at around eight to ten months, and happens when the baby becomes extremely distressed when their 'attachment-person' leaves them. This can even extend to the mother (or father) not being able to go to the toilet without the baby becoming distressed and desperate, leading to an upsetting situation for parents as they feel that they have absolutely no private space. This is when the baby needs calm, firm handling. Getting angry and frustrated is understandable but try not to take these negative feelings out on the baby, it will only make things worse and the stage of insecurity will only be prolonged. This stage will soon pass, but is more likely to be positively resolved if parental reaction is firmly and calmly containing. By the time the baby reaches true toddlerhood, this depth of separation anxiety will almost certainly have eased up.

Even if your toddler is outgoing, friendly and confident (and separation appears to be relatively painless), there will inevitably be stumbling blocks at times. They are still emotionally very fragile and immature and, at times, seemingly minor events can throw a spanner in the works! The birth of a sibling, a parent having to be hospitalised, a little friend hurting her at playgroup – all these (and many more) can be the triggers that cause regression and a resultant sense of insecurity and clinginess. I will discuss some stressful toddler situations in the next chapters. However, suffice to say that it is then necessary to go back a few steps and handle the anxiety as discussed previously. Becoming impatient and punitive will only make things worse. Understanding and empathy, balanced with gentle firmness, is the balance to strive for and in fact, the only strategy that will encourage a return to more confident separation. The vital fact is that separation is a slow process that cannot be too hastily accelerated.

THE PROGRESSION FROM TODDLER TO PRE-SCHOOLER

Between the ages of two and four (the true toddler stage), an enormous amount of physical and emotional growth takes place. By approximately four years old, the toddler should be well prepared for longer periods of separation and ready for more structured activities, which will gradually prepare her for the requirements of Grade 1. At the tender age of two, the emphasis should not be on structured 'learning' (sitting the toddler down and 'instructing' her) but rather be geared towards pure play, slowly moving to learn the basics of socialisation. For this reason it is always advisable to introduce the toddler to very age-appropriate social situations in the form of Moms and Tots groups, small playgroups or play dates with one or two other toddlers.

Activities should be varied and stimulating, and expectations age-appropriate. The setting and programme should be flexible and non-rigid and, most importantly, any person to whom you entrust your toddler should be child-centred and approach discipline according to the principles outlined in the foregoing chapters.

Toddlers need to feel free to explore, try out newly-developed skills and feel encouraged to be creative and spontaneous, all within the safety of clear, consistent and firm (yet gentle) boundaries. The following quote from How to Parent by Fitzhugh Dodson says it very well. (The word 'mother' in his quote can be replaced by anyone who cares for toddlers.)

"In the Age of Exploration, the most priceless gift you can give your toddler is the freedom to explore. This will require patience from you as a mother. You will surely have impatient moments with a house that looks at the end of each play day as though a windstorm had hit it. But remember that those beautiful, well-manicured houses you see, which look as if no children lived there, cannot possibly be homes for developing children with feelings of self-confidence. When a mother has a toddler in the house, she can basically make one of two choices. She can choose to have a spotless house and raise a toddler full of self-doubt. Or she can choose to have a periodically littered house and raise a toddler full of self-confidence. If you make the second choice, you will give your child the best possible send-off into his next stage of development."

SUMMARY OF CHAPTER 15

- Toddlerhood is the transitional stage between babyhood and childhood. This means that it is characterised by ambivalence, with the toddler veering between the need to cling like a baby and then become independent and rebellious.
- Parents feel ambivalent too – longing for space and freedom, yet feeling sad and confused when their toddlers appear not to need them.
- Temperament plays an important role too. Some babies seem to be born confident, while others are clingy and anxious.
- The anxious/shy toddler needs acceptance and understanding, and parents should avoid over-pressurising and premature enforced separation. Verbalise their anxious/ fearful feelings, while simultaneously avoiding becoming over-anxious yourself. Gradually encourage the toddler to learn resilience and coping strategies.
- Do not remove security objects too hastily or harshly.
- When it is necessary to go back to work soon after the baby's birth, choose the closest option to one-on-one home-care. Make sure that you receive support and input to deal with any negative feelings you may have.
- Separation anxiety is a normal aspect of child development. The more closely a baby is allowed to cling and have basic needs met, the more secure they usually feel, resulting in easier separation at a later stage. Try not to react angrily and negatively if your baby or young toddler goes through a stage of pronounced clinginess. Patient firmness usually ensures that this phase passes relatively easily.

- Handle separation in the older toddler by going slowly. Choose play and toddler groups with care and introduce your child gently. Avoid prolonged farewells, as this only exacerbates the separation problems.
- Remember that the toddler stage should be a time of relaxed exploration and creativity, within appropriate and consistent boundaries. A Toddler Group is not a 'school'; it is a *play*group. Toddlers need one-on-one adult care, and input and discipline that is gentle yet firm, taking all relevant toddler needs and developmental characteristics into account.
- If the toddler is well handled, he will be optimally ready to move into the pre-school stage.

16

Maintaining boundaries in stressful situations

COMPROMISED COPING MECHANISMS

Parenting is an enormous challenge. Parenting a toddler is an even greater challenge. And parenting a toddler when challenging, stressful and traumatic life experiences occur, is an even greater challenge.

Toddlers are particularly vulnerable and impressionable, as they are still so totally dependent on the security and stability of adults. They have undeveloped coping skills, only basic communication ability and limited ability to understand the ups and downs of life in any logical or rational sense. This dependence places additional strain on parents during stressful times, especially if their coping mechanisms are compromised.

You don't have to be perfect

It becomes an enormous challenge to provide secure physical and emotional boundaries so necessary for the toddler's development, when parents find that their own boundaries are inconsistent and uncertain. During these challenging and stressful times, it is encouraging to remind oneself that toddlers do not need perfect parents or, in fact, perfect life circumstances. They do very well with 'good enough' parents.

Many parents come for counselling because they feel burdened by guilt – they had hoped that life would be easier and that they would be in a position to give their children an easier, less complicated and happier childhood. But life is unpredictable and throws many a curved ball, so it is very important to remember that children are amazingly resilient, and that the ups and downs of a challenging childhood can add to this natural resilience.

> **It is not so much the event itself that affects children, but the adult reaction to the event. Therefore, it is of huge importance that parents find appropriate help and support during these inevitable life crises.**

The events that parents most commonly express concern about are the following:
- The birth of a sibling.
- Conflicting parenting styles, including the influence of grandparents.
- Moving house.
- Hospitalisation of a parent or the toddler.
- Separation, divorce and step-parenting.
- Death.

Each of these could be a book in itself. What follows is a brief overview in order to give the parents of toddlers some of the 'tools' to assist with the implementation and maintenance of appropriate boundaries.

THE BIRTH OF A SIBLING

There is no ideal age-gap between babies and, as much as parents may try to plan their families as carefully as possible, things do not always go to plan! It does appear that the 'norm' seems to be approximately a two-year gap between the first and second baby. If one acknowledges what the two-year-old toddler is coping with developmentally, and then add to that the stress and trauma of being replaced by a younger sibling, it is no wonder that families often experience quite a challenging time of adjustment.

The toddler is unable to think rationally. This means that, no matter how carefully, clearly and repetitively mom and dad put their toddler's little hand on the 'bump' to 'feel the new little brother/sister in Mommy's tummy', a two-year-old is not capable of visualising a growing baby. At that age, it is simply a case of 'seeing is believing', so it is unsettling when (as seen through the eyes of the toddler) Mommy suddenly disappears and returns a few days later with this new little 'usurper'.

To visit, or not

Parents are often confused as to whether or not the toddler should be taken to the hospital to see the new baby. They may feel concerned that the separation (when toddler has to say goodbye to Mommy) could be worse than staying in safe and familiar surroundings until mom comes home. My own view is that it is better for the toddler to visit Mom. The emphasis should be placed on the toddler having the chance to see that Mom is okay and has not disappeared completely, with the baby very much the 'understudy' in this particular scene! The separation from Mom needs to be handled as outlined in the previous chapter – gently and firmly, with positive distractions immediately available. However, you are the best judge of your own toddler. If you believe the experience will be too traumatic, follow your gut feelings and opt for the non-visiting option. In either event, the following are some basic tips:

- Allow for a time of insecurity and clingy behaviour following the return from the hospital. She was the centre of the family's 'universe' but now her world has been turned upside down. Not only has she had to cope with her mother being away, but when she did return, she was tired and physically fragile. And, to top it all, she has brought home this demanding newcomer.
- Wherever possible, allow someone else to hold the baby so that you can reassure the toddler that he is still very important to you.
- Make feeding times as calm and special as possible and try to include the toddler. Either make this a time to feed the dolls/teddies as well or allow the toddler to sit close to you while you read her a story. I still remember, with such warmth and happiness, the time after my second daughter, Samantha-Jane was born. Her older sister, Catherine, was 22 months old, and loved sitting next to me and the baby at feeding time, 'breastfeeding' her special teddy as she clutched it firmly to her chest. She included all the necessary paraphernalia too: the cloth nappy for burping, the cushion for resting an arm on, wet wipes and nappies for emergencies!

- When friends and family visit, ensure that they make a fuss of the toddler. It is so easy, in the excitement of seeing the new baby, for people to forget about the sidelined toddler.
- Remember the importance of decoding behaviour. The ignored toddler may very well behave badly, as this is the only way she knows of expressing her feelings of rejection and jealousy. Verbalise the feelings, in this way helping her to feel that, even though her behaviour may be unacceptable, her feelings are understood.
- Do, however, keep the boundaries firmly in place. "I can see that you are feeling left out, but we do not throw our toys when we are cross." Follow up with a clear choice, and enforce the consequences. "If you throw another toy, you will have to go and sit in the quiet corner." Then follow through – even if someone has to gently (but firmly) accompany the angry little person.
- Do not make exceptions or excuses for the unacceptable behaviour. "He is feeling so out-of-sorts since I brought Sophie home, but we feel we should just ignore the bad behaviour for now." This will only lead to manipulation and more serious, ongoing problems later.
- Beware of developing unrealistic expectations. This toddler is not suddenly 'a big sister or brother' overnight, just because there is now a younger child in the house. Parents can so easily fall into the trap of expecting the older child to suddenly become more reasonable, understanding and helpful. She is, in fact, still a little toddler, with all the developmental challenges typical of this stage to cope with. Take it easy on her, and do not neglect her enormous needs for emotional support at this very stressful time in her little world.

CONFLICTING PARENTING STYLES

In my twenty-six years of working directly with parenting issues, I cannot recall a single occasion when both parents agreed 100% on issues of discipline. Even in families where the parents share the same philosophy regarding child raising, there will be differences in perception and application. It is important for parents – especially during the earlier childhood years – to understand that it is not their differing viewpoints that are potentially damaging and divisive, it is the fact that their children learn to manipulate the differences between them. One parent may say to their two-year-old: "Hannah, the toys need to be put away before we play in the garden," and, when Hannah refuses, the other parent (in order to avoid the inevitable power-struggle) says, "Don't force her, she's only two. She can play outside and I'll tidy the toys!"

What lessons is Hannah learning?

- She can get her way by making a fuss, because her 'softer' parent will come to her rescue and save her from the 'strict' one.

- That when the 'strict' parent and the 'soft' one enter into the ensuing argument, a smokescreen is thrown up and the actual event is forgotten. A very helpful lesson in the art of manipulation for the future!
- And, very unfortunately and sadly, that she is more powerful and important than one of her parents. A psychologically unhealthy 'alliance' is then formed between parent and child, with the other parent becoming sidelined and earning the 'bad parent' label. This is not a positive sign for the future inter-relationships in this family.

Many parents have then asked the very valid question: "But what happens if I sincerely cannot support the punitive and harsh discipline methods of my partner?" This is a very sensitive issue. It goes to the very heart of the state of the parental relationship. Remember the earlier chapters and the emphasis placed on the need to work on positive communication between the parents. Also the statement that a positive relationship between her parents is the best 'gift' a child can be given. And add to this the need to discuss issues of parenting styles and discipline methods **before** these evolve into serious problems later.

However, in those cases where there are already power struggles, accusations, labelling, you-messages and disconnections, the following are some helpful tips:

- Never criticize your partner in front of your toddler. The only exception (hopefully an extremely rare one!) would be if a child is being abused by another adult.
- Try to support the other adult, even if this is very difficult due to the fact that you and your partner view discipline differently. Perhaps you think it unfair and unrealistic to expect a two-year-old to pick up her toys, but when your partner gives the instruction to do so and the toddler resists, instead of causing a division, say, "Your mom asked you to pick up the toys. Let's see who can pick up the most toys."
- When one of you firmly believes in the benefit of that 'one good smack' and the other is determined to avoid the smacking trap, the best option is to stick resolutely to your purpose. Refrain from criticism and 'preaching', but rather let your own, more positive approach to discipline, be the role model needed to show concrete proof of the negatives inherent in the 'smacking habit'. Each parent must inevitably take long-term responsibility for the type of relationship forged with each child. When children pull away from an over-strict and autocratic parent, it is the direct result of the parent's approach to parenting. When the two of you have quiet time, away from the eyes and ears of impressionable toddlers, use your positive communication skills to address these differences. Rather than saying, "You should never smack Justin again. You are just like your father and look how scared you were of him," try saying, "It distresses me to see Justin becoming afraid and anxious. The last thing we want is for him to have a relationship with you based on fear, like you had with your dad!" This is the power of non-judgemental I-language!

- Be honest regarding the core issues around your disagreements. Very often, disconnections in a relationship are already evident before the parenting issues take central stage. These then become the 'excuse' for avoidance of real, deeper issues.

A frequently asked question regarding grandparents

"What do I do when our own parents interfere regarding our child-raising methods?"

In my first book, *Children Need Boundaries*, I devoted a chapter to the issue of grandparenting, so will not repeat the entire contents here, suffice to say that this can become a potential mine-field, and one which (once again) those very intuitive toddlers can very quickly assess, and use to ultimate advantage!

Important points and helpful hints:

- The first words of caution go to grandparents: remember that these are **not** your children. They have their own parents, who have the right to parent their children as they choose, just as you did. Times have changed and society has different expectations, challenges and stresses than it did thirty, forty or fifty years ago. My favourite quote from Kahlil Gibran's *The Prophet* seems very appropriate here:

    "Your children are not your children. They are the sons and daughters of life's longing for itself. They come through you but not from you, and though they are with you – yet they belong not to you. You may give them your love but not your thoughts, for they have their own thoughts. You may house their bodies but not their souls, for their souls dwell in the house of tomorrow, which you cannot visit, not even in your dreams. You may strive to be like them, but seek not to make them like you. For life goes not backward nor tarries with yesterday. You are the bows from which your children as living arrows are sent forth."

- This is also especially for grandparents: try to listen more than you speak. Give advice only when asked, and then do it tactfully, emphasising I-language. "I feel concerned when I see that Tammy does not have structured meal-times." And **never** criticize the child's parents directly to the child, even if you think they are too young to understand!
- Now for parents: Remember to put yourself in your own parent's shoes. The world, and especially the way children are parented and disciplined, has changed dramatically. Also remember that it becomes harder to change your mindset, the older you get. Be patient and avoid harsh criticism and other negative communication.
- Avoid personal attacks on each other's parents. This will only lead to defensiveness and counter-attacks. "You say my mother is too indulgent, but yours is so cold and strict. The children hate going there." What possible good can come of this type of

accusatory language? Remember that children's birthright includes their right to the best possible relationship with *both* extended families.

- Obviously, if there are legitimate problems with grandparents, then use your mature, calm and assertive communication skills to tackle the issues. Make a time to sit quietly to address any perceived differences or difficulties. "I know you love spoiling Amy and we really do appreciate the time you spend with her, but if you would rather bring her healthy treats instead of sweets and chocolates, we would be so grateful."
- Allow grandparents' rules to be implemented in their own homes, but then expect the same when they visit yours. Children are quick and very receptive to the differences. As long as the rules in each situation are consistent, they will be fine. "I know Grandpa lets you put your feet on his sofa, but here we don't do that."
- Issues become more complicated when a child's parents live with their own parents or in-laws. This can be a minefield of resentment and confusion, which is clearly disastrous for effective parenting. Whose rules apply here? What rights do the toddler's parents have?

My advice here is to try to settle differences via family meetings and cool, clear adult heads. If it is the grandparents' home then their house rules must be viewed respectfully, but the children need to understand that their parents have primary responsibility for their discipline. Drawing up lists, making time for reviews, clarifying roles and responsibilities and sharing grievances before they erupt, will all assist in the establishment of productive methods of conflict resolution, and open lines of adult communication which will optimally assist in the ultimate goal of positive parenting of toddlers and children.

SOME GENERAL TODDLER STRESSES

Many situations, which do not appear stressful to older children and adults, can be immensely traumatic for toddlers:

- Being taken to a new playgroup.
- Having a new nanny or carer.
- Losing a security blanket.
- A parent being unexpectedly hospitalised.
- The toddler being hospitalised or ill.
- A parent going away for a time.
- Moving house.

All these, and many more, can cause immense distress to a toddler. Their sense of security and safety depends so totally on the adults in their lives, that any disruption of the routine and predictability in their lives can have enormous repercussions.

We have covered all the most important parenting strategies and skills already, but let's highlight those that maximally assist a stressed and disorientated toddler:

- Never minimize or suppress the toddler's feelings. "It's just a silly blanket. We can find another, nicer one."
- Empathize warmly and lovingly. "It's very sad when a special blanket gets lost." This won't bring the blanket back, but it will help this little person feel understood and that he is allowed to feel upset.
- Remember all the advice in Chapter 15 regarding coping with separation.
- If one parent has to be away suddenly for whatever reason, ensure that the other parent, or an adult the toddler is well-bonded with, is able to keep the routines and structures as close to 'normal' as possible.
- If a toddler has to be hospitalized, do not become over-anxious and begin preparing the child too soon, as this will only exacerbate the anxiety. However, never avoid some sort of preparation. I remember reading the 'horror stories' of some misguided attempts at preparing children for operations like tonsillectomies. The parents said something like, "Let's pack a suitcase and go for a little picnic," and then took the child straight to the hospital and got her prepped for the operation, before she actually realized what was happening! Fortunately, most parents today know better! Even though a two to three-year-old cannot fully understand what's going to happen, reading simple stories about going to hospital and playing 'hospital games' (with the routine which is likely to be involved being role-played as a fun exercise) is good preparation before the 'real thing'. This all helps to alleviate the levels of stress, and of course, most hospitals today encourage an adult that the toddler trusts to be with the toddler immediately before (and after) the procedure. In most cases, the hospital will actively encourage a parent to remain with the toddler in hospital.
- These situations are also greatly helped if the toddler has 'attached' to a security object. Packing that special teddy or 'blankie' and adding a scarf that smells of Mom (or Dad's handkerchief) gives the toddler a concrete reminder of the important adult. These kinds of items also help in situations where the family moves home. As long as the familiar objects are clearly visible, and quickly unpacked, the toddler will immediately feel safe and secure.

The most important aspect of all the stressful situations that life might have in store for the toddler is the way in which the important adults in her life handle the challenges!

When adults are okay and find positive ways to cope, the children are more likely to be okay too.

THE IMPORTANCE OF DECODING SKILLS

The physical and emotional safety and security of toddlers is defined and determined by the choices and reactions of the important adults in their lives. They are totally dependent and unable to make decisions about events and situations that impact directly on them. The only way in which they can manifest their feelings of confusion, insecurity, sadness and anger, for example, is to behave unacceptably. It therefore becomes very important for empathic adults to learn decoding skills. As outlined throughout this book, this means the following:

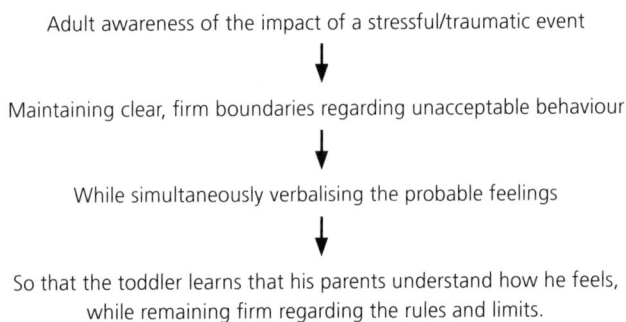

Adult awareness of the impact of a stressful/traumatic event

↓

Maintaining clear, firm boundaries regarding unacceptable behaviour

↓

While simultaneously verbalising the probable feelings

↓

So that the toddler learns that his parents understand how he feels,
while remaining firm regarding the rules and limits.

In the final section of this chapter, I will highlight some issues involved in helping toddlers to cope optimally with divorce and death. Once again, I have already devoted a chapter to this in my *Children Need Boundaries* book, so this will be a somewhat cursory overview.

Two of the most stressful events in anyone's life are death and/or divorce. Although babies and toddlers are obviously too young to understand the full impact of these devastating events, it is important for parents to be aware of the possible long-term ill-effects of poor decision-making during these times of stress in families.

17

Toddlers and divorce

South Africa's divorce rates are sadly amongst the highest in the world. This means that thousand of children, of all ages, are negatively affected by the disintegration of their primary source of support – the nuclear family. In my private practice, and in my role as school counsellor, I deal with (on a daily basis) the impact of divorce on children. Parents constantly ask me if there is a 'best case scenario' when it comes to the age of children at the time of divorce. This is akin to the question: "How long is a piece of string?" There simply is no ideal age. Children are always negatively affected but, as stated at the beginning of Chapter 16, it is the adult reaction to stressful events that will primarily determine the impact on the children.

The bottom line is that children develop a type of radar system in order to ascertain whether the world is safe or not. Even babies are finely tuned to the emotional vibes emitted by the adults around them. Babies and toddlers may not be able to make sense of the tension and acrimony that they begin to pick up on those toddler-type 'radar screens'. They just know that all is not well with their protectors and nurturers, and this will have repercussions for their development of trust and autonomy – so vital for their healthy psychological development.

Some guidelines for divorcing parents of toddlers

- It is most important to seek professional help. Find support and opportunities to vent away from the children. This will help you to be as calm and capable as possible when you are dealing with your young children.
- Remember that feelings are an integral part of being an emotionally intelligent person. Feeling sad, resentful or angry cannot be totally avoided. Even a two-year-old can be told, "Mommy is feeling a bit sad," or, "Daddy is not feeling happy right now." This will ease the need to get out their little radars. Body language is stronger than words, so if you look sad but say you are okay, their radars will have to work overtime to try and make sense of your non-verbal cues. Toddlers are extremely egocentric. If you say something simple like, "Mommy is sad because Daddy isn't here," your toddler will feel relieved that she hasn't caused the sadness, and she will be able to turn off the radar because your words confirm what she is picking up.

- Never overburden your toddler with your intense adult feelings. She certainly does not need to know the intricate details of the problem. Say just enough to be open and honest, but then pack the issues away in your 'adult suitcase' and try to keep things as normal and calmly contained as you possibly can.
- Always remember that children deserve, in fact have a right to, the best possible relationship with both parents. You may be angry and resentful towards your partner, but your child has two parents, and will be more likely to emerge from the trauma of divorce as psychologically intact as possible if you are able to constantly bear this in mind. A very hurt, sad and angry father said to me recently, "At times I wish their mother would just disappear. But I know they love her and she will always be their mom, so I must try to get over my rage and move on for the sake of my beautiful children."
- Remember that you will have to co-parent your children for a very long time and that you are equally important in the lives of your children. The sooner you can work towards a reasonably positive working relationship, the better for all concerned.
- Toddlers need structured and predictable routines. It is not conducive to their sense of security to have some sort of loose and flexible contact-plan. "I feel it best for the kids that their father comes to see them at my home whenever he can. He phones and I try to be as amenable as possible." As good as this may sound to the adults, it is not helpful for children. They need to get into a structured contact-routine as soon as possible.
- Most available research on the best contact arrangements for children under the age of three, points to the need for shorter, more frequent contact with the non-primary parent (the one with which the child spends less time). In other words, rather an hour or two each day than a whole day, once a week. Or you could try two hours on two afternoons a week plus four hours one day over the weekend. Obviously, the times should be increased as the toddler adjusts to the changes.
- Many people have the false belief that, because toddlers are so young and haven't yet formed entrenched ideas about family structure, they will adapt more easily than an older child would. In fact, it could be even harder for toddlers. They are still forming their primary attachments and find it very stressful to be away from either parent for long periods of time. Therefore, having to move from one parental home to another can be extremely stressful and needs very insightful and gentle handling. Also, at this tender age, a child has no ability to think abstractly. If Mom and Dad are not visible, it is as if they don't exist, whereas an older child is able to visualise the absent parent, which provides a measure of comfort. This is another example of a situation where security objects become indispensable.
- Even very young toddlers love having a visual depiction of when they will see their parents. Making a monthly calendar for the toddler to have on their bedroom wall, with Mom's

days in one colour and Dad's in another, is an excellent aid. Toddlers also love 'counting sleeps': "It's two more sleeps until you see Daddy," or, "Just one more sleep until you see Mommy." This type of clear structure helps children feel safe and contained.

- Never say negative things about the other parent, no matter how much you feel justified in doing so. This is destructive and will only lead to children feeling the need to develop elaborate defence mechanisms. In young children, this takes up enormous amounts of emotional energy, which are actually needed for the developmental challenges of their age and stage.

- Although there is no doubt that positive maternal bonding is a vital step in a baby's early development, paternal bonding is just as vital. Toddlers are often very attached to their mothers, which is why it has been the norm to award custody of babies and toddlers to their mothers, with fathers often having to accept the 'every second weekend and Wednesday afternoons' access settlement. With the new Children Act 38 of 2005, this has changed dramatically. The word **custody** has been replaced by **co-care and responsibility**, and the word **access** by **contact**. This essentially means that parents are now viewed, in the eyes of the law, as being of equal importance to their children. Also, that both parents should have a role in determining important decisions regarding their children.

- The challenge, in the case of babies and toddlers, is to find child-centred ways in which to positively encourage the healthy bonding process between the child and both parents. Although there is no longer the legal issue of sole custody, one parent will usually be awarded 'primary residence', especially in the case of young children. The idea is then to draw up an age-appropriate, gradually accelerating, contact plan. This is to ensure that the child's right to an equal relationship with both parents is assured. With this mindset, it becomes an issue of power sharing and co-parenting, and not one of one parent having more power to determine what is best for the children. This makes it less likely that children (especially the very young ones), will become pawns in ongoing parental 'wars' involving acrimony and tension, which only exacerbates feelings of instability and insecurity in the vulnerable children involved.

- Each parent needs to develop clear and consistent rules and boundaries. Neither has the right to tell the other parent what those should be. One parent may feel strongly about not eating in the lounge, while the other is more easy-going. The only aspect that could be detrimental to a toddler would be openly disagreeing or criticizing. However, if it is possible to have calm and mature discussions (usually best in a neutral place) about important aspects, such as the use of sun-screen, no fizzy drinks or too many sweets, using car-seats and seat-belts etc, this can only be beneficial.

- It is essential that both parents are able to balance their roles: to be a firm, consistent boundary-setter as well as an empathic nurturer. Traditionally, mothers were the nurturers and fathers the disciplinarians. When divorce happens, moms then find themselves as the nurturers and boundary-setters, and dads become the fun, mostly weekend parents (especially under the old access laws) and feel reluctant to discipline during their infrequent times with their children, thereby becoming the indulgent parent who cannot bear to deny their children any request! With a stronger emphasis on more equal time, this will hopefully change so that both parents will nurture and provide age-appropriate limits and boundaries. This is also a case for an altered mindset on discipline. In other words, if parents see discipline as loving and positive limit-setting and not as harsh and angry smacks and shouting, it becomes easier to be fun-loving and kind while still saying, "No," to requests for those extra treats.

- Remember, the extended family is still very important too. Just because you have unresolved issues with in-laws, is no good reason to refuse permission for your toddler to visit them. They are still, and always will be, your child's grandparents.
- Finally, it is always a positive decision to appoint a professional facilitator – someone who will assist with the re-establishment of communication channels, and who can give advice that is in the children's best interests when parents become embroiled in power struggles. Toddlers are unable to verbalise their distress and therefore are also unable to benefit, in any meaningful way, from even the most toddler-centred play therapy. However, having an appointed facilitator, well trained in child development and psychology and who can speak on behalf of the toddler, is immensely beneficial, both in short and longer terms.

Life after divorce

Children, including little toddlers, can be incredibly accepting and resilient. Divorce is unfortunate, but life does go on and toddlers do learn to cope with the changes and disruptions. They can adjust to almost anything – it is usually the parents who find it more daunting! The most important post-divorce issue for toddlers is for each parent to establish as smooth and predictable a routine as possible when the child is in their care. They can adjust remarkably well to the transitions, as long as they are allowed some leeway for adjustment. If parents get divorced when their children are still in the baby and toddler stage, it usually means that one (or both) of them will form new relationships.

A word to unmarried parents

Exactly as in the case of divorced parents, toddlers deserve the best possible relationship with both parents. In the days before the Natural Fathers of Children Born Out of Wedlock Act of 1996 was promulgated, mothers had total control of the type of relationship fathers were allowed to have with their 'illegitimate' children. Mothers had legal custody and guardianship, although fathers had to pay maintenance – even in cases where they were continuously denied access! Thank heavens that the rights of the child are now paramount.

It is very important that, right from babyhood and toddlerhood, single parents realize how crucial it is for children to be allowed to know about their biological fathers. I have been amazed at the illogical thinking of mothers I have counselled who have sincerely believed that it is better for a young child to grow up thinking that their step-dad is their 'real' dad. The confusion and anger experienced later, when an older child finds out the truth of his paternity, is hard to imagine! Therefore, right from the start, if the 'real' dad is not around for whatever reason, never collude with the toddler's innocent acceptance of another 'dad' as their biological father. Children will develop primary bonds with the person who fulfils their 'father' role, but should nonetheless never be denied the true facts of both their parents.

A postscript to this is obviously that the same applies to adoption. Babies and toddlers will not understand the concept, but if adoptive parents become comfortable with using the word 'adopted' from the beginning, there will never have to be a decision about that 'moment of truth'. If parents say words like, "You are my special adopted baby," then later, to a two-year-old, "We were so lucky to adopt you," the pre-schooler will then one day ask, "What does 'adopted' mean?" And, because you have used the word constantly, you will be able to answer easily and truthfully. Once again, it must be emphasized, that it is your open, easy and truthful responses to potentially stressful situations, which will minimize the potential for escalating problems.

A FEW TIPS RELEVANT TO TODDLERS AND NEW PARENTAL RELATIONSHIPS

- Allow the toddler time to get to know the new person. 'Slow and sensitive' is a good motto to remember. Toddlers need to develop trust in new relationships, and this takes time and patience.

- If you are the parent having to let go, so that your toddler can build bonds with your ex-spouse's new partner, this can be excruciatingly painful. However, it is impossible to halt this inevitable stage of the post-divorce process, and putting up too many obstacles will only cause stress for your toddler. You only have a right to raise objections if you have factual evidence of neglectful or abusive treatment of your child. You have to keep remembering that your ex loves his/her child and would not allow a partner to harm the toddler. The best way to cope is to ensure that the process accelerates gradually: start with shorter times and, as the toddler adjusts, increase the time accordingly.

- If you are in the 'step' role, take it very carefully and tactfully. It is a good idea to request a 'coffee and chat' with the other parent, in order to reassure him/her that you are not trying to take over the role of biological parent, and that you would be very open to any reasonable advice or suggestions. This can only be beneficial to all concerned, especially the toddler.

- However, right from the word go, ensure that both of the toddler's parents accept that you will be in loco parentis, meaning that you have a role in boundary-setting and rule enforcement. Even very young toddlers very quickly learn where they can manipulate situations. When their developing 'radar systems' tune into the fact that Mom clearly does not like Dad's new wife and is very ready to undermine her at any opportunity, the switched-on little toddler will work the system to her best advantage!

- If you find yourself in the role of step-parent to a toddler, and you have absolutely no parenting experience, it is highly advisable to seek parent skills counselling, attend a workshop and/or find appropriate books on the topic. Parenting is a challenge and step-parenting is even more so.

- When the toddler becomes resistant or distressed at changeover times, it can be extremely distressing for everyone, but this can be a normal result of toddler separation anxiety. Handle the situation according to suggestions made in Chapter 15. The important issue is not to allow the toddler's distress to become a reason to deny contact with the other parent. The best solution is the careful and empathic manner in which the toddler has been encouraged to separate from one parent, and to bond positively with the other. Added to this is a quick and tension-free 'handing over'. Lingering, going back for extra hugs and kisses, or – worst of all – using the handover time for heated debates or acrimonious exchanges, will only prolong the agony of the separation. Usually, once the toddler has settled with the other parent, the tears and tension will be over and the toddler will settle happily. However, if the toddler becomes inconsolable and is clearly becoming too traumatised, then the other parent should be called. At times like these, a special belonging of the absent parent; a soft scarf or a handkerchief, even a jersey with Mom or Dad's 'smell', can become a sense of reassurance and familiarity to the toddler.

TODDLERS AND LOSS

At any stage during childhood, the loss of an important person is distressing for the child. Divorce causes an enormous sense of loss, which is why children have often shared with me that the feelings they experience are as if someone has died. There is therefore a pervasive sense of grief when the family is broken. Of course, loss caused by death is immensely traumatic. For a child in the stage of toddlerhood, the very fabric of the newly-acquired sense of trust is totally destroyed if a parent dies. This is not only because of the devastating physical loss, but also the ripple effects in the family caused by the grieving process.

There is no way the family can insulate the children from the effects of grief and loss. Toddlers have no ability to make sense of the sudden changes and the sense of insecurity caused when all their familiar routines and rituals are no longer as predictable and structured as they were. The loss may be of a sibling, parent or grandparent and the impact on the toddler is the inability of the trusted adults to provide the safety and security that was in place prior to the crisis.

Some important points to bear in mind during times of serious crisis – which could include the effects of violent crime:

- Try to ensure that the toddler is in the care of a trusted adult who is capable of taking care of the toddler's basic needs. A word of caution here: It would be wonderful for a bereaved toddler to be fortunate enough to have a loving grandparent to step in when a parent dies, but the grandparent needs to remember that he/she will never be the parent, and that the surviving parent will need to re-establish their pivotal role in the future parenting of the child. It is often easy for a grandparent to take over the role of parent during the time of grief and trauma, which could make it difficult for the parent to regain a primary role in the child's life. Over-reliance on the grandparent could also pose a problem in the event that the parent forms new relationships with possible future partners. This becomes a case of re-establishing positive boundaries as soon as possible after traumatic events.
- If possible, try to keep the toddler's familiar objects accessible: special toys, duvet cover, familiar books, DVDs, and of course, as many security objects as possible.
- You will have to make allowance for clingy and insecure behaviour. The toddler will

almost certainly regress – especially if a parent dies. Allow this. The toddler will need all the close connectedness available in order to be capable of regaining a sense of trust and security.

- Although the toddler may show signs of sadness and confusion when faced with reminders of the lost loved one (like photographs), it is a mistake to remove all the reminders, although some of the more emotionally painful objects should be stored safely away for a time when the toddler is capable of communicating more adequately. I remember a little boy who was brought to me for counselling many years ago. He was nine and his mother had died very suddenly when he was four. In a well-intentioned attempt to protect his son from daily reminders of his mother, the father took away all the photos and albums. This very distraught boy shared with me, through his pent-up grief and confusion, how he had longed to see photos of his mom and that, when his father had removed all those precious reminders, he had battled to retain the memories of her. As he got older, he thought that his dad could not bear to see the photos, so he never mentioned them. Replacing the photos and having the albums to refer to, was a painful therapeutic process that brought healing for both father and son – five years after the tragedy. Although a two-year-old is still a baby, removing photographs and other reminders is sometimes done to protect the child, but in fact, it is often actually done to protect the adult.

- A tragic loss is that of a child. A great deal can be written about this, suffice to say that there can be very little worse than this for parents and extended family. The ripple effects on the surviving children, no matter how young they are at the time of the loss, can have far-reaching effects on their lives. All the above points made about the loss of a parent apply here too. It is crucial that the surviving sibling/s are dealt with sensitively and supported as empathetically as possible, so that they do not feel overlooked or sidelined. Many children I have counselled, following the death of a sibling, have shared with me that they began to feel very guilty that they could never replace the child who died. They tend to internalise, often incorrectly, that they have to try to make up for the loss, but that somehow, nothing that they do can ever be as good as their sibling would have been. This needs very skilled professional assistance.

All the above-mentioned stressful events will impact on the toddler's sense of security and the need for structure, predictability and calm consistency. However, crises and change are all an integral part of life. Handled with appropriate care and skill, these stressful events will help your toddlers develop coping skills which will enhance their sense of resilience and adaptability for all those curved balls that life is sure to have in store for them.

SUMMARY OF CHAPTERS 16 AND 17

- Parenting is challenging at the best of times. During stressful and challenging times, it is enormously difficult to effectively parent a toddler.
- Family crises impact on children of all ages. Toddlers, who have fragile foundations of trust and security, are particularly vulnerable, mainly because they are still so totally dependent on the important adults in their lives.
- The thread that runs through all the stressful events that affect children is that it is the *adult reaction to the event* that has the biggest impact on how the child will cope with it. Simply put, if adults are okay, children will more likely be too.

COMMON COPING STRATEGIES FOR STRESSFUL EVENTS

- Parents should seek adequate professional support, guidance and input.
- Ensure that the toddler has a capable, coping adult that they trust to maintain a sense of routine and predictability.
- However, bear in mind that no one else can be the child's missing parent. Grandparents are a very positive asset during this traumatic time, but they can never take the place of a parent, therefore boundaries need to be re-negotiated as soon as possible.
- The loss of a sibling needs very sensitive handling as the surviving child can feel guilty, and can also feel that they have to make up for the loss during their childhood years.
- Allow the toddler to regress to a degree – they often need the clinginess of babyhood in order to regain confidence and trust. Encourage the use of familiar security objects.
- Try to maintain the security of limits and boundaries, while simultaneously decoding unacceptable behaviour and verbalising the feelings that are causing the behaviour.
- In cases of divorce, the key to handling toddlers is to remember that he has two parents who are equally important in his life, and that bonding with the non-primary parent relies on regular, predictable contact. This contact should be gradually, age-appropriately accelerated.
- The way in which parents cope with stressful events has a direct correlation to the long-term effects on the children. No one needs a perfect parent – 'good enough' parents will do. Crises happen, mistakes are made, and children survive. The critical difference between merely surviving and developing into a resilient, capable, confident and well-functioning adult, relates directly to the ability of the parents to cope as positively as possible with stressful situations.

Epilogue

There can be no doubt that the toddler stage is crucially important for the establishment of positive parenting skills, which will help to lay the foundation for future discipline patterns.

There can also be no doubt that the toddler stage is exhausting, both physically and emotionally. After the challenges of the adjustment to parenting, and the attempts at regaining a sense of equilibrium as the newborn becomes a settled baby (and then a determined and energetic toddler), the focus needs to shift back to the exhausted and disorientated parents. Due to their egocentricity and drive towards control, toddlers can drain parents of every grain of energy, spontaneity and confidence that they may have had in those far-away pre-baby days. This can be equated to a petrol gauge in a motor vehicle. Parents, especially mothers, get into the habit of running very close to 'empty'. Metaphorically speaking, it becomes a case of rushing from filling station to filling station – putting in just enough fuel to keep going until the gauge is close to empty again. However, once in a while that gauge needs to move to the 'full' end of the dial!

"Kids can give energy back to us, but for the most part it is right and proper that **we recharge them**. However, when we are their only source of refuelling and we dry up on them, something is bound to happen. Think for a moment. Where is your energy tank right now?

Is this where you usually keep it? Are you always running on empty? We often treat our bodies as we treat our cars! Ten dollars worth at a time, bald tyres and long overdue for a tune-up!"

Steve Biddulph: *The Secret of Happy Children*

Therefore, as mature and intelligent parents, it becomes a priority to look after your own personal development and to find positive ways to nurture your adult relationships. It will not serve the best interests of your children if you strive to be perfect parents, but in the process become totally burnt out and therefore unable to function as well integrated individuals. This will then almost certainly lead to a disconnection in your relationship with your partner. What good will your perfect parenting skills be to your children if you become alienated from each other?

It cannot be emphasized strongly enough just how important it is to fill up your emotional tanks on a regular basis. So, here are some suggestions:

- Never view it as depriving your toddler when you are able to organise 'time out' from the rigours of parenting. I rate looking after oneself right at the top of the list of parent effectiveness skills. Over-developed parental conscience can, in fact, do more harm than good. Remember that children need happy, fulfilled parents.
- Remember that you do not atrophy as a growing and developing person just because you become a parent. Your needs for self-actualisation are important and can be realized alongside your development as an effective and well-balanced parent.
- Toddlers do not need perfect parents; 'good-enough' is all they need. You *will* make mistakes, and hopefully, learn from them. Your good intentions, realistic expectations and positive communication skills will keep the lines of parent-child interactions healthy and open.
- Maintain a sense of humour. Parenting is challenging, but it can be fun, creative and spontaneous. Run, laugh, dance, play, draw and paint with your children. Life can be serious, so keep it light and try not to take it all too seriously.
- Being a parent is a most wonderful opportunity for personal growth. Toddlers help to tone down tendencies to be over-controlling, too strict or too serious. They help us see that an untidy house is not a crisis; muddy footprints do not mean war and a flooded bathroom floor (after a fun-filled bath session) can be mopped up quite easily!
- Most importantly, reconnect with your partner. Find time to talk, share and listen. Show that you still care. Remember the fun you had before you had children? Those days aren't over – you can still have fun times. They may take more planning, but will be well worth the effort. So fill up those adult fuel tanks!
- **Never allow having children to become an excuse not to nurture your relationship with your partner.**

The reality is that you can have children – with all the concomitant challenges and adjustments – as well as a fulfilled and satisfying relationship, both with yourself as an individual, and with your partner.

Good luck with all the challenges that coping with toddlerhood brings. It is a most exciting and rewarding time. Enjoy it, with all its highs and lows. Before you know it, your toddler will be a pre-schooler – and the process of separation and independence will be well and truly underway. And you will think fondly back to those days of tantrums, lost security objects, power struggles over eating and potty training, endlessly taking her back to bed, and be amazed that it all seemed so intense at the time! Make the most of every precious moment because it will be history in no time at all.

"Scott Peck writes, in The Road Less Travelled. (1978). 'It is only because of problems that we grow mentally and spiritually. It is through the pain of confronting and resolving problems that we learn.' Benjamin Franklin said, 'Those things that hurt, instruct! Problems do not go away. They must be worked through or else they remain, forever a barrier to the growth and development of the spirit. I can solve a problem only when I say, "This is my problem and it's up to me to solve it". Love is the will to extend oneself for the purpose of nurturing one's own or another's spiritual growth. We do not have to love. We choose to love.'"

Alison Osborne: *The Post-baby Conversation*

Bibliography

Biddulph, Steve. 2000. *The Secret of Happy Children*. Harper Collins. Australia.

Cawood, Anne. 2007. *Children Need Boundaries. Effective Discipline without Punishment*. Metz Press. Cape Town.

Corkille Briggs, Dorothy. 1975. *Your Child's Self Esteem*. Doubleday Co. Inc. New York.

Covey, Stephen R. 1999. *The 7 Habits of Highly Effective Families*. Simon and Schuster. London.

Dodson, Fitzhugh Dr. 1974. *How to Parent*. WH Allen and Co Ltd. London.

Faber, Adele and Mazlish, Elaine. 1999. *How To Talk So Kids Will Listen and Listen So Kids Will Talk*. Picadilly Press. London.

Faure, Megan and Richardson, Ann. 2007. *Sleep Sense*. Metz Press. Cape Town.

Gibran, Kahlil. 1985. *The Prophet*. AD Donker (Pty) Ltd. Craighall.

Ginott, Haim. Dr. 1969. *Between Parent and Child*. Crosby Lockwood Staples. London.

Goleman, Daniel.1996. *Emotional Intelligence*. Bloomsbury Publishing PLC.

Leach, Penelope. 1994. *Children First. What Society Must Do – and is not doing – for children today*. Penguin Books. Middlesex. England.

Meyer, Moore and Viljoen. 1990. *Personality Theories from Freud to Frankl*. Lexicon Publishers. Johannesburg.

Osborne, Alison. 2007. *The Post-baby Conversation*. Metz Press. Cape Town.

Rowling, J.K. 2004. *Harry Potter. The Chamber of Secrets*. Bloomsbury Publishing PLC.

Turecki, Stanley Dr. 1995. *The Difficult Child*. Judy Piatkus. London.

ARTICLES

Buckley, Helen. 1998. *The Little Boy*. Centre for Conflict Resolution. University of Cape Town.

Hunt, Jan. 1995. *Ten Reasons Not To Hit Your Kids*. Reprinted by permission of EPPOCH (End Physical Punishment of Children).

The Parent Centre, Positive Parenting Manual: Skills for South African Parents. Cape Town.

Centre for Conflict Resolution. 1998. Peace Education Manual. University of Cape Town.